After
Callimachus

The Lockert Library of Poetry in Translation

Series Editors: Peter Cole, Richard Sieburth, and Rosanna Warren

Series Editor Emeritus (1991–2016): Richard Howard

For other titles in the Lockert Library, see the list at the end of this volume.

After Callimachus

Poems

Stephanie Burt

Foreword by Mark Payne

Princeton University Press

Princeton and Oxford

Requests for permission to reproduce material from this work
should be sent to permissions@press.princeton.edu

Published by Princeton University Press
41 William Street, Princeton, New Jersey 08540
6 Oxford Street, Woodstock, Oxfordshire OX20 1TR

press.princeton.edu

Library of Congress Cataloging-in-Publication Data

Names: Burt, Stephanie, 1971– author. | Callimachus | Payne, Mark (Mark
Edward), writer of foreword.
Title: After Callimachus : poems / Stephanie Burt; foreword by Mark Payne.
Description: Princeton : Princeton University Press, [2020] | Series: The
Lockert library of poetry in translation
Identifiers: LCCN 2019051812 (print) | LCCN 2019051813 (ebook) | ISBN
9780691180199 (hardback ; acid-free paper) | ISBN 9780691201917 (ebook)
Subjects: LCSH: Callimachus—Adaptations. | LCGFT: Poetry.
Classification: LCC PS3552.U7695 A68 2020 (print) | LCC PS3552.U7695
(ebook) | DDC 811/.54—dc23
LC record available at https://lccn.loc.gov/2019051812
LC ebook record available at https://lccn.loc.gov/2019051813

British Library Cataloging-in-Publication Data is available

Editorial: Anne Savarese and Jenny Tan
Production Editorial: Ellen Foos
Text Design: Leslie Flis
Jacket/Cover Design: Leslie Flis
Production: Erin Suydam
Publicity: Jodi Price and Katie Lewis
Copyeditor: Richard Smoley

Jacket/Cover Credit: Jacket art: 1) Background mosaic: Shutterstock. 2) Inset: Detail
of dog-headed Mercury as symbol of November. Roman (c. 3rd century AD),
formerly at Thrysdus. Sousse Museum, Tunisia © Ad Meskens / Wikimedia
Commons

The Lockert Library of Poetry in Translation is supported by a bequest from
Charles Lacy Lockert (1888–1974)

This book has been composed in Minion Pro text with Gotham Narrow display

Printed on acid-free paper. ∞

Printed in the United States of America

10 9 8 7 6 5 4 3 2 1

Contents

2

3

4

7

Foreword

Callimachus is the greatest Greek poet you probably haven't read. He stands at the head of a list of writers from the third century BCE who were to transform the way that poetry was written and appreciated in the Greek-speaking world and the Roman literary culture that succeeded it. Some of these names are familiar: Theocritus, because of the influence of his bucolic poetry on Vergil's *Eclogues* and later European pastoral, and Apollonius, whose *Argonautica* has remained in view as a minor classic of epic literature. Others are less well known: Aratus, whose poem on the constellations was assiduously emulated by celebrity translators at Rome, including the statesman Cicero, and Germanicus, heir apparent to the emperor Tiberius, or Nicander, whose poem on transformations is the proximate model for Ovid's *Metamorphoses*.

The surge of admiration that greeted Callimachus's work in the ancient world is in stark contrast to his lack of modern admirers. Callimachus never found his ideal translator, as Homer found Chapman, Pindar found Hölderlin, or Propertius found Pound. Perhaps this is not so surprising. For the ancients, Callimachus was an innovator, reinventing the past from a position of quizzical distance. For moderns looking to the Greeks for a model of what it is like to be embedded in ancestral forms of life, Callimachus is no use at all. Like us, he is an anthropological adventurer in antiquity, embracing the distance that makes his own work possible.

Callimachus was born in the Libyan city of Cyrene and spent his working life in Egypt, at the court of the Macedonian dynasts who ruled the newly founded city of Alexandria. He is supposed to have compiled the contents of their Royal Library, producing a catalog of over one hundred volumes. With access to a mass of archival material that had been gathered into one place for the first time in the history of the Greek-speaking peoples, Callimachus could see more of early Greek life than anyone who had actually lived it; presumably for this very reason, he saw it ethnographically. He made no attempt to synthesize his archival discoveries into a universal vision of Greekness. Just the opposite, in fact. His most famous poem, the *Aetia*, is a four-volume collection of curiosities from the Greek world at large, spliced with poetic theory and polemics, and enlivened with episodes from his own life.

An *aetion* is a cause, or a reason why things are the way they are, and its plural, *aetia*, gestures at a collection of *just-so* stories—a big book of explanations, probably boring. Yet Callimachus is anything but a painstaking burrower after encyclopedic certainty. His love of knowledge is a child's enthusiasm for discrete fact sets in all the glory of their first discovery. Putting them into poetry as such is, he tells us, *the way of Apollo*, a style of composition the god taught him when he was little, and which he perseveres with as an adult. In Stephanie Burt's version, this foundation document of poetic license reads:

> So reactionaries and radicals complain
>   that I have no proprietary mission,
> no project that's all mine;
>   instead, I am like a child flipping Pogs
> or building in Minecraft, although I'm past forty.
>   To them I say: keep rolling logs
> for one another, but don't waste my time
>   on your ambition:
> marathon runners and shock jocks gain
>   by going as far as they can, but the sublime,
> the useful, and the beautiful in poetry
>   are all inversely correlated
> with size. Shorter means sweeter. I'll be fine.
>   When first I rated
> myself as a writer of some sort,
>   wolf-killing, light-bearing Apollo came to me
> as a ferret. Stay off crowded trains, he said; never resort
>   to volume where contrast will do. Imitate
> Satie, or Young Marble Giants. The remedy for anomie
>   lies in between the wing slips of the cicada.

Only fragments of the *Aetia* remain (some, like this one, quite substantial), but what held it together was the figure of the poet himself. A century earlier, Aristotle had praised Homer for not making a spectacle of himself in the *Iliad* and *Odyssey* and letting his characters do the talking for him, but Callimachus is all over the *Aetia*, which is all about being Callimachus. Stephanie Burt gets what is going on here as no translator has before. At a certain age, we start to feel embarrassed by the things we care about. A child keeps her rock collection where everyone can see it, but an adult stores hers in the attic, or heaves it in the garbage with a sigh. But what if we could get over our middle-aged embarrassment at the small enthusiasms that animate our lives? What might our embarrassment turn into if we brought our enthusiasms out into the open, with a gesture of unabashed avowal? If the point of collections is to share them, what if we kept on sharing them past forty, as Apollo told us to?

> Why do I write? Experience
>   and scientific evidence agree:
> an otherwise intolerable load
>   of shame decreases by up to six percent
> if told to even a temporary companion,
>   through a folded-up page at recess, a performance
> on classical guitar, a palinode,
>   a Tumblr, or a hash mark on a tree;
> fears diminish, at least a little, whenever secrets
>   are no longer secrets and enter the common
> atmosphere, even as birdsong, even in code.

Callimachus's new and distinctive voice emerges with particular clarity in Stephanie Burt's translation of this poem. On the one hand, we see Callimachus the well informed nonfiction writer who put what he learned about Alexandria's incipient technologies to good poetic use. The research institute of which the Library was a part oversaw great leaps forward in medicine and the applied sciences, and Callimachus himself is credited with prose works on winds, rivers, and birds; local names for fishes and the months; and the historical foundations of various islands and cities. We also see Callimachus the master of verse, a supreme technician at making Alexandria's novel forms of discourse at home in the demanding metrical forms of ancient Greek poetry, of which he employed an unprecedented variety.

Think back to Plato's *Symposium*. Socrates and Aristophanes debate the reasons why the same person cannot write tragedy and comedy. Poetry must be a kind of inspiration, not a kind of craft; otherwise the same person could learn to be good at both. Aristotle has his own version of this story in the *Poetics*: back in the day, tragedy corralled the talents of high-minded folk, comedy of the low, and to this very day, he says, the same people do not write both. Callimachus will let these just-so stories out the back door. He wrote narrative poetry in the hexameters of Homer (*Hecale*), instructional poetry in the elegiac meter of the classical moralists (*Aetia*), poems celebrating the gods in the mode of the Homeric Hymns, victory odes like those of Pindar, city foundation poems (*ktiseis*), a kind of poem that became wildly popular amid the imperialist land grabs of the Hellenistic era, *Iambi*, a scurrilous and personally vindictive kind of poetry that had fallen into desuetude by the time Callimachus took it up again, and epigrams, short-form poems with lines in alternating meter that also became enormously popular in the period.

Callimachus transformed some of these forms so radically as to make them virtually a new kind of poetry. His *Iambi*, for example, open with bringing Hipponax back from the dead, but this most foul-mouthed and degenerate of all the ancient poets is unrecognizable in his zombification. He lectures his new audience serenely on the virtues of mindfulness and getting along together. The rest of the collection contains poems spoken by plants, a birthday song by a child god, and reflections on the role of aniconic statues in deep history. His miniepic, *Hecale*, focuses on humility and unexpected moments of kindness. His Hymns showcase dazzling panoramas of primordial Greek landscape, the Olympians as children, and feats of narrative prestidigitation not guessed at by the ancient hymnists.

Of this fountain of excellence, some poems reached modernity in their entirety in a regular manuscript tradition—the epigrams and Hymns—while the rest have had to be reconstructed and reimagined from citations in later authors, or papyri recovered from the sands of Egypt. Modernist poets reveled in the imaginative possibilities of the minimal fragment—especially the erotic fragments of Sappho— and Stephanie Burt works her own magic with the scraps of Callimachus. Consider this two-line fragment from *Hecale*, for example, in my own literal rendition (fragment 274):

ἁρμοῖ που κἀκείνῳ ἐπέτρεχε λεπτὸς ἴουλος
ἄνθει ἑλιχρύσῳ ἐναλίγκιος
A light fuzz was just getting going on that youth
resembling a golden flower

Callimachus is Instagramming the links in a traditional image bank here. *Anthos* means something that comes out of concealment to play upon a surface where it is now visible—"anything thrown out upon the surface, eruption," according to Liddell and Scott's *Greek-English Lexicon*, hence flowers, foam, and facial hair. For the Greeks, this is an inherently positive experience. Bloom is a coming into one's own, a self-realization. In the process of human maturation, the appearance of facial hair is when sexual attraction makes itself felt for the first time, and this is a moment of extraordinary poignancy for both the subject and their beholder, hence this hair's resemblance to a golden flower in the poem—a precious, epiphenomenal instantiation of desirability.

All of this we know—"it's part of the culture"—but look at what Stephanie Burt does with this knowledge. From the exiguous fragment of *Hecale*, she conjures a whole transhistorical drama of becoming male:

Honestly I don't know
    if he'd want me to say so,
but I love how he has just
    now started to grow a beard—

I could tell from the delicate hair —no, the down
    on his cheek. I thought of the tips
of the petals of the Italian immortelle
    which are, also, gold.

I could see, when he blushed,
    his pride, his satisfaction
(he had been waiting so long for it):
    he had just shaved.

It's an expansion, obviously, but not in the mode of bloviation, and we should pause for a moment to consider what it means to be able to expand so successfully on a poet who valued concision as much as Callimachus did. The fragment has regrown itself from its damaged stock, and become the thing it was always meant to be. We see more in the original than we could have seen without the expansion, but seeing more does not violate the integrity of the original. The translation brings out the truth of the original. It is the bloom of its hidden being.

If I had to guess, I would imagine that Stephanie Burt acquired this power of efflorescence from her apprenticeship to the epigrams, which predates this collection by over a decade. Through long acquaintance with the explicit, she has acquired a kind of fluency—confident, yet always considerate—in drawing out the latent. Listening in, as trusted confidante, also allows her to capture the elusive voice of childhood that sometimes makes its presence felt within the self-assured professionalism of Callimachus the public intellectual. In the breathless midsection of the *Aetia* prologue, for example, what it felt like to know things as a child still sparkles at the poem's surface, like a golden fuzz that won't stop showing.

There is a gestural quality to the way that Callimachus's poems enact their commitments. You can feel the poems heating up in places, as the childhood core of his inspired technique reveals itself in hot spots on their smooth Apollonian face. One might think of Cy Twombly in this regard. His canvases are populated by sparse, gestural indications whose facture, Roland Barthes observed, is "a little childish, irregular, clumsy." Barthes used the Latin term *rarus* to characterize Twombly's way of working. In Latin, *rarus* is "that which has gaps or interstices," what is "sparse, porous, scattered." Barthes's language of sensuous appreciation goes all the way back to Callimachus. What Barthes calls "rareness" in Twombly is what Callimachus called *leptotes* in his own work. It is a thinness, or lightness of touch, at the level of a work's gestural surface, by which the work communicates that the enthusiasm in which it originated is not exhausted in its own execution. The beard of fragment 274 is a *leptos ioulos*.

The genius of Callimachus's style resides in such inimitable occasional gestures. His private conversations with the gods, his raptures over some pair of star-crossed lovers he has dug up in an obscure volume of local history, his conversations with a house guest about the weird folkways of their homeland—these are marked as both the persistence of childish enthusiasm and the supreme realization of his art. When he leads us to believe that his enthusiasm for what he knows is about to betray him into revealing some terrible secrets about Hera's childhood amours with her brother Zeus, he stops himself midflow to tell us that too much learning is a dangerous thing. It's hard to shut up about it, so you're always in danger of injuring yourself with the thing you're in love with, like a child with a knife (*Aetia* 3.75.4–9).

Callimachus being Callimachus is hard to resist, and even harder to imitate. Critics and admirers, ancient and modern, have all too often scraped the icing off his poetic cakes, preferring to chew on the dry mix of his book learning instead. Consider for a moment an actual child poet from antiquity. At the Capitoline Games of 94 CE, the Roman child Q. Sulpicius Maximus earned an honorable mention in the competition for verse improvisation for his extempore effusion on the words Zeus might have spoken when chiding Helios for lending his chariot to Phaethon. The poem is preserved as part of a commemorative inscription of Sulpicius's early death by his grieving parents, and what they praise is his precocious attainment of adult skills, rather than anything distinctively childlike about his performance. Little Sulpicius ran through his whole project without stumbling, even though he was only eleven years old. He was a cause of wonder because he could already do what adults do.

Callimachus, on the other hand, does just like a child. He works on a small scale, going as slowly as possible. He does not improvise ("I sing nothing unattested"), and he belabors his own uncertainties and missteps ("I am like a child with a knife"). Callimachus is an antiprodigy, his poetics of childhood a refusal to be the kind of child that adults like to see when they are looking for the adult in the child rather than the child in the adult. It is this linkage of adult craft skills with a retained child mind that drops away in Callimachus's Roman admirers. They admire him as a supremely skilled poetic craftsman, but do not appreciate that these skills are being used to operational- ize the freshness of beginner's mind, a child mind that continues to see the world and know things about it as if it were seeing and know- ing them for the very first time. Here he is, for example, on the early history of the Greek cities of Sicily:

> The settlers came from Kume and Khalkis,
> led by the captains Perieres
>   and Krataimenes, who called himself the Victor
> (he had good reason, given where he'd fought).
>   No sooner did they land in Sicily
> than they began to erect, and to fortify, walls;
>   they never laid the herb mesh, nor did they spread the celery leaves
> that would have kept off the harpies,
>   or else attracted a heron to chase them away.
> You on the mainland have probably never seen
>   harpies, and lucky you if so:
> their shadows shelter slanderers; the trails
>   their filthy feathers turn children sad
> or disobedient, and seeds to sterile dust
>   before they're sown. Those same birds' iron talons
> buckle pavements, and—adding injury
>   to injury—their presence makes routine maintenance
> next to impossible: nauseated citizens
>   refuse to pay their tax—

mistrustful and badly nourished, they can't see past today.
    If you ever have the misfortune to launch a colony
do not settle where the harpies land.

This is one of Callimachus's city foundation narratives, a reflection on the historical experience of the early Greeks. The style of mind is paratactic. There is no obvious attempt to impose a principle of organization on the material, or to subject the historical forms of life portrayed to an intellectual or critical agenda. The childlike absence of filter populates Callimachus's historical imagination with a superabundance of detail, yet it is this very exaggerated, childlike refusal to subordinate that captures the weirdness of historical life as it is actually lived:

    And so even now, even on sacred days,
the city, its peacock markets, and its docks
    so close to the bourse, its reciters and lutenists,
seed vendors, rhetoric teachers, and resident priests
    refuse to say the name of either man.
In fact, they prefer to avoid even naming the town,
    whose name on maps means something like "sickle" or "scythe."
When the deputy mayors announce
    the annual civic feast, they say,
"May the majestic initiators
    of our metropolitan way of life—
whoever they were; we really have no idea,
    it was so long ago—grace our revels and green our fields;
we honor whatever they did or might have done."
    They roast at least two oxen, and their round cakes,
though slightly burnt, taste sweet, with basil and lime.

A gnostic disquiet stalks these visionary scenes. Callimachus's commitment to the craft of the poem overrides the framing of its contents, allowing the weirdness of the historical record to live and breathe and walk around in the poem *on its own terms*. Imagine being born into such a world! But so we are. Only a god knows why we live this way, but there it is, a dark wonder for our contemplation. Child mind plus supreme craft equals a new kind of poetic apparatus. It allows for a conjuring, rather than a mere imagining, of the past.

Baudelaire said that for the child "everything is new, he is always excited," but the flip side of this excitement is the claustrophobia of being thrown into a world that is too full of what is already there for the child to feel at home in it. In the face of everything that presses in upon him with its demands for recognition, his powers of engagement desert him, and he withdraws in sullen resentment, unable to process:

> You've been my friend for a while. You know you can trust me.
>   You know I consider education worthwhile.
> And now that you're teaching middle school
>   for who knows how long, I'd like to help you see in it
> something more than a divine punishment.
>   You're going to smolder inside, sometimes. I know.
> We all have. It's an archaic frustration. But if
>   the fire inside you isn't a firestorm, won't
> burn forests to charcoal, and needs to be put down,
>   just tamp it down yourself. Try to hold your horses,
> rather than chasing them more than once
>   around their own track. You'll just end up cracking your skull
> on the first tight curve. Some lesson that would be,
>   and nothing new.
> Don't laugh at me and I won't laugh at you.

Callimachus can imagine culture as playground and prison. For this poem's schoolchildren, there is no outsider perspective to which the poet-historian might deliver them at recess, no Apollo hovering in the background to bless the work in hand as a task of self-realization—no erotics of knowledge, just a more or less well-behaved resistance trying to make it through the day. Perhaps it is this all-too-familiar feeling of ennui that gives Callimachus's love poems their all too familiar feeling of overinvestment in emotional rescue, their gravitational pull toward whatever might break though the atmosphere of boredom:

> Half of me—an intangible half—is alive;
>   the other part has gone I don't know where—
> either it's dead, or it's lost in what it calls love.
>   Actually it's a flighty tween,
> superficial and glittery. "Keep your eyes
>   on the printed page; stop playing with your hair,"
> I tell it, "and put down your portable screen!"
>   No use. I'm supposed to profess
>   that maturity is a gift,

but I don't believe it, or else don't care.
    I amble the library stacks and get lost in YA;
I want to go home, paint my nails until they iridesce,
    clamp on my headphones, and pray to Taylor Swift.

Where the *Aetia* gleefully documents the fusion of pleasure and labor in bringing the archives of Alexandria to life, short poems like this one reimagine the traditions of Greek epigram as inscribed verse. Behind the epigram's painful arithmetic of addition and subtraction—x number of Spartans overcame y number of Persians at a total cost of z to themselves and their loved ones; x number of animal A was sacrificed to gods B, C, and D, in order to acquire benefit y for polis z—Callimachus recovers the labored effusions of erotic graffiti, Greece's earliest graphisms. Attraction multiplies and divides, and Callimachus's hypertrophic bookkeeping of desire and its travails shows all the workings of this erotic calculus, the splittings and recombinations of desirous clusters of selfhood that express what it is to have gender and to be sexed for others.

In his backward gaze, Callimachus hailed the ways in which the early Greeks had pioneered this knowledge, framing out a mythopoetic space his contemporaries could finish for themselves. And of all the things Stephanie Burt has realized about Callimachus, perhaps none is more urgent for our historical moment than the Greek poet's understanding of how our commitments to particular forms of care, concern, and desire direct us to inhabit the embodiment of others in ways that may not be true to their own self-experience. In his Athena hymn, Tiresias, the Eternal Trans of the Greek tradition, is, first of all, the object of a mother's love, a mother whose emotional certainties the goddess must work upon with an injunction to look harder, to be more attentive to how it is that she thinks she knows him:

        If you want to know about blindness
    ask someone blind. Your son
        can see everything you see. But he can't pay attention,
    because he's also seeing times to come.
        It's like having all
    of everything, each pebble and sprig, each spray
        of rain or sun, press down on him at once.
    He will know the past and the future.
        But he will need to be led from place to place.

In ancient Greek poetry, divine knowledge is often imagined as the possession of a different cognitive range, the ability to hold in the mind's eye a massive array of particular details beyond the scope of ordinary mortals—not the insight that can see the world in a grain of sand, but the supersight that can attend to every grain of sand in the world *on its own terms*. This, as we have seen already, is Callimachus's way of knowing, and his Tiresias, like the poet himself, belongs in the company of Apollo, the subject of his second Hymn, just as much as he belongs in the company of Artemis and Athena, the refusers of prescribed forms of womanhood who are the subjects of his third and fifth Hymns. All of this Stephanie Burt understands and appreciates as no one has before. This is Callimachus for real, a poet for our time, and for all time, who we can catch up to, and catch on to, at last, thanks to Stephanie and her superpowers.

Textual Note

The most readily accessible Greek texts of Callimachus are the Loeb Classical Library editions, which are available in both print and digital form. The Greek and English texts of the digital editions are fully searchable, and the format matches that of the print books, facilitating comparison. Susan Stephens's edition of the *Hymns* (Oxford University Press, 2015) is an inexpensive bilingual edition with excellent notes. Annette Harder's edition of the *Aetia* (Oxford University Press, 2012) has also been consulted, although this magisterial two-volume set of the fragments, with translation and commentary, will be prohibitively expensive for the common reader. The numbering of the Hymns is consistent across editions, and this is mostly true of the epigrams too. Numbering of the *Aetia* and *Iambi* fragments is more variable. The numbers in this translation are those of the Loeb edition, but the first line of the Greek text has been provided for all of the poems translated except the Hymns, so they can be readily identified in any edition, past, present, or yet to come.

Mark Payne

Imitator's Note

These pages reflect, interpret, adapt, respond to, and sometimes simply translate the poems, and parts of poems, that the ancient poet Callimachus wrote. They were composed in Greek, on the southern coast of the Mediterranean, in or near Alexandria, under the Ptolemaic rulers of what is now Egypt, in the third century BCE. By no means do we have access to all that he wrote. What we do have has come down to us through quotations in later writers, through the luck of manuscript preservation (in the case of the Hymns and Epigrams, whole preserved books; for other poems, fragments), and through what archaeologists have found in the scrap heaps and rubbish holes of antiquity (most of all the famous rubbish holes of Oxyrynchus). I have tried to do justice to what this poet of Hellenistic antiquity says, to how it feels to read him, to his characters, to his locales, to his gods.

At the same time the English verses in this book should not be mistaken for consistently accurate scholarly translations. Such translations already exist. Some of the English here closely imitates or directly translates Callimachus's Greek. Much of it does not. In adapting Callimachus's surviving complete poems and (even more so) his many fragments, I have made cuts, expanded on his metaphors, provided new metaphors, fleshed out situations he leaves implicit, imposed other situations whose modern details the original Alexandrian could not have imagined, based English phrases as much on the sounds of the Greek as on its literal sense, and sometimes aggressively modernized his world.

If this book is a work of translation (and I hope it is!), it's also science fiction, or alternative history. My goal has been, not a historically and linguistically precise reconstruction of his poems in their original Alexandrian and Hellenistic contexts, but rather a new Callimachus in contemporary English, a poet who feels at once close to the Greek original and like a fresh, coherent, wise, entertaining, and sometimes even humorous poet writing in mostly American English for readers today.

Callimachus—my Callimachus—lives in a world with twenty-first-century technology, though his world is not our own. He and his coevals fly on airplanes, send email and Tweets, and rely on modern medicine: they know synthetic hormones, tractor trailers, video games, reverb pedals, Olympic compound bows. Some of them even watch *Star Trek*. Artists and musicians who exist in our world have counterparts in this one, and they go by the same names (e.g., Mahler). Political history in Callimachus's world may resemble the history of our own (as in Epigram 8). But political geography does not. He and his coevals live in a world of Mediterranean city-states: there is no America, no sub-Saharan Africa, no New Zealand, and all the place-names here come from the Mediterranean, unless I made them up.

Callimachus and his coevals also live in a world of Greek polytheism: the gods of Olympus, and the gods of local river systems that feed the Aegean, are real to their worshippers and may well confer favor or displeasure. Nobody knows, in his world, how real these gods are (they do not appear and make miracles for human beings, or at least not any more), but they are real in his poetry, and they are real figures of worship for the (imaginary) people in his world, the readers of his poems, just as they were for the earlier classical authors—Homer, Hesiod, Simonides—who show up in Callimachus's original Greek as well as in these English-language poems. Callimachus worships Artemis and Apollo, and sometimes Athena—the latter two are sponsors of his craft, and of the urban civilization that keeps him safe and feeds him, but he may feel closest to Artemis, icon of skill and erotic fulfillment and wildness, and of adventure in a world without adult men. Callimachus also pays necessary homage to Zeus, of whom nobody should speak ill; admires Demeter for her role in feeding the world and caring for households; and maintains a complicated, ambivalent relationship to Hermes and Hera.

I have enough Greek to read, with help, the original, to understand its syntax and morphology, to know what words are related to what other words, what nouns are unusual, what verbs are common, and so on, though not enough Greek to teach an introductory ancient Greek course or to succeed in a PhD program in classics. You would not want to rely on me for an accurate literal translation, from scratch, of a Greek poem that no one had translated before. But Callimachus has been translated more than once by scholars who aim for literal versions, and I have consulted previous translations; I have relied on friends (especially Mark Payne), on Annette Harder's *Aetia*, on Susan Stephens's *Hymns*, and especially on the prose versions of Callimachus in two volumes of the Loeb Classical Library, prepared and translated by A. W. Mair and C. A. Trypanis. Without their work this book would not be possible.

"I'm not over-fond of Greek meters in English," quipped the nineteenth-century poet James Russell Lowell. I have not attempted to replicate them, let alone to copy Callimachus's own. I have, however, tried to make metrical patterns in English that do some of the work I hear in the Greek. The sonic patterns in many of these poems, with their high proportion of triple feet, are, I hope, not so rigid as to sound forced, not too close to any famous English-language model, and regular enough that readers can recognize their recurrence from poem to poem. (They have—if I got it right—a great-aunt or uncle in Louis MacNeice's *Autumn Journal*.) Making up for the absent complexities of the metrical patterns in the Greek original, many of the short poems here use rhyme.

More than a decade ago, the poet and scholar John Talbot called Callimachus "one of the great missed opportunities in our literature." Susan Stephens adds that his displays of learning, his allusiveness and his syncretism, are "not the pose of a cynic," but "may stem from the complexity of the task that the poet has set himself, namely, to explore the potential for cultural interactions for which there was not, as yet, a corresponding reality" (Stephens, *Seeing Double*, 114). To adapt, or imitate, Callimachus as I have attempted to do here is to engage in more such explorations: I hope that mine are remotely worthy of his.

I am grateful to the journals and anthologies that first published some of the imitations and translations here, sometimes in differing versions: *American Scholar, Aotearotica, At Length, Columba, Brink, Iowa Review, Kenyon Review, London Review of Books, Paris Review, Plume, Thumbscrew, Tikkun,* and *Yale Review.* I also thank Graywolf Press for permitting the republication of four poems from *Parallel Play* and four from *Advice from the Lights.*

Callimachus was, in addition to everything I have said above, a poet who wrote in a port town, of ships and the sea, seeing them off and hoping for their return. May you take pleasure in these words, as I have done; may they guide you to further travels and further adventures of your own.

Further Reading

Bruno Snell's chapter on Callimachus in *The Discovery of the Mind* (Dover Publications, 1982) is a classic of unparalleled insight into the poet's relationship with earlier Greek literature and culture. More recently, Alan Cameron's *Callimachus and His Critics* (Princeton University Press, 1995) transformed the perception of Callimachus as a cloistered, bookish, ivory-tower *litterateur* into a public intellectual embroiled in the culture and political affairs of his time. For more on Callimachus, his Alexandria, and its relations to the wider cultures of Egypt and of Greece, see Susan Stephens' monograph *Seeing Double: Intercultural Poetics in Ptolemaic Alexandria* (University of California Press, 2003). One of the few contemporary studies of English-language reactions to Callimachus is John Talbot, "English Ghosts of Callimachus," *Arion* 12:1 (2004): 139-170; Talbot's essay incorporates his review of another translation, Frank Nisetich, *The Poems of Callimachus* (Oxford University Press, 2001).

Readers of Helen DeWitt's *The Last Samurai* will be familiar with the auratic charm of P. M. Fraser's three-volume *Ptolemaic Alexandria* (Oxford University Press, 1972). Newer treatments exist, of course, but DeWitt's novel testifies to the sustained magic of Fraser's deep dive into the life of the ancient city. Roland Barthes's two essays on Cy Twombly and the art of gesture were lightning rods for my own understanding of Callimachus's poetics of childhood (*"Non multa sed multum,"* and "The Wisdom of Art," reprinted in *Writings on Cy Twombly*, edited by N. Del Roscio, Schirmer/Mosel, 2003). Mark Golden's *Children and Childhood in Ancient Athens* (Johns Hopkins University Press, 1990) was the foundational work for the study of ancient children; Susan Langdon's paper "Children as Learners and Producers in Early Greece" in *The Oxford Handbook of Childhood and Education in the Classical World* (Oxford University Press, 2013) contains invaluable new information on the life and work of child ceramic artists in antiquity.

1

(*Aetia,* book 1, frag. 1: proem)
Οἶδ᾽ ὅτ]ι μοι Τελχῖνες ἐπιτρύζουσιν ἀοιδῇ

So reactionaries and radicals complain
    that I have no proprietary mission,
no project that's all mine;
    instead, I am like a child flipping Pogs
or building in Minecraft, although I'm past forty.
    To them I say: keep rolling logs
for one another, but don't waste my time
    on your ambition:
marathon runners and shock jocks gain
    by going as far as they can, but the sublime,
the useful, and the beautiful in poetry
    are all inversely correlated
with size. Shorter means sweeter. I'll be fine.
    When first I rated
myself as a writer of some sort,
    wolf-killing, light-bearing Apollo came to me
as a ferret. Stay off crowded trains, he said; never resort
    to volume where contrast will do. Imitate
Satie, or Young Marble Giants. The remedy for anomie
    lies in between the wing slips of the cicada.
If I can't be weightless, or glide among twigs, or sate
    myself on dew, then let
    my verses live that way,
since I feel mired in age, and worse for wear.
    It might even be that when the Muses visit
a girl, or a schoolboy, they intend to stay,
    or else to come back, even after the poet goes gray.

(*Aetia,* book 3, frag. 67–75)
Αὐτὸς Ἔρως ἐδίδαξεν Ἀκόντιον, ὁππότε καλῇ

This is a story with a happy ending.
　　If you met Aaron early enough in his life
you might have wondered who taught him the arts
　　　of conversation, he who could put anyone,
adult or child or
　　　in between, at ease,
yet got tongue-tied when he brought up Cydippe,
　　he who wanted nothing more than to see her,
in fact, to spend the rest of his life beside her,
　　so that the world would see him as her husband.
They had a lot in common. The two of them met
　　　at Delos, at the big sacrifice; he came
all the way from Iulis. They would talk
　　about how both of their mothers were engineers,
how both had family in the islands,
　　about the races outdoors, about where to stand
to avoid the crowds at the temple.
　　But already other sons' mothers regarded her
as the prize, bringing bride-gifts, bringing whole oxen,
　　although, in her own eyes, she was far too young.
Nobody else stood out in the morning dances;
　　nobody else reminded
so many observers of the rose-gold dawn.
　　He stood out too, but frankly
it made him uncomfortable.
　　More than uncomfortable. You might have heard
he spelled his name differently then. People singled him out
　　in school, and at parties, back home. He liked the attention,
but only at first. He got really into archery,
　　and all of us thought he just liked spending time in the sun.
In fact he was praying
　　to Artemis, to the thin moon
he observed after dawn, and right before sundown:
　　praying she might see him,
that Cydippe might see him, the way
　　he so badly wanted to be seen.

That the proverbial archer might strike her too—
       not Artemis nor Apollo: the other one. That it might hurt
just a little. That they could talk about his prayers.

       And that's just what happened. "I think you're brave," she said.
"I don't think you deserve to be afraid."
       Bad news: by then her mother had arranged,
of course,
       for Cydippe to marry someone else.
Good news: our heroes got to spend
       the night together first, because the cult
of Hera insists—
       I'm going to get in trouble, serious trouble,
if I go into detail here. Just know
       that families in Hera's cult insist
on this kind of bridal evening. For the education
       of daughters, who will then make better wives.

       Next morning the families led
two oxen to the pool where they would see
       the point of the blade that would tear their hearts out that night.
That's part of the Hera cult too. But that afternoon
       Cydippe had a fit. A literal fit,
the kind that makes people behave like wild goats,
       flailing and barking. They thought she was going to die,
and canceled the ritual. And then she got better.
       And then the ceremony was back on,
at which point she came down with a boiling fever,
       which lasted seven months. As if she had worked for it.
And then she could breathe again, so they set the wedding
       for a third date, and then she came down with a chill,
more than a chill: a frost fever, so her very lips
       and eyes seemed to congeal, as if she could not
remain for long in this cold world . . .

       At this point Cydippe's father knew enough
to pray to Apollo, who came to him that night.
       "My sister will not permit this marriage," said the god.
"She was right there in her shrine, though you did not see,
       at the festival in Delos,
when your child swore that Aaron, and nobody else,
       would be her husband. Yes, her husband.

And now, if you care for your daughter, you'll listen to me.
    For one thing, she swore an oath, and she's bound to keep it,
and my sister agrees." The god
    reached over his shoulder, grasping
one of his sun-bright arrows. Artemis, too,
    can shoot such radiant arrows with perfect aim,
though hers look more like moonlight. "For another,"
    the sun god went on, "if you let her marry Aaron,
you will not blend lead with silver,
    but rather mix your silver with his gold.
You know your own stock. He comes from mountain climbers,
    and from wind tamers; his family taught
their island to catch quail in wind-borne nets."

So Aaron came back to Naxos, and the girls
    whom Artemis befriended said their hymns,
including the marriage hymn, over both of them,
    and Aaron, for all you love to hunt and sprint
and shoot, I know you would not
    have traded that night for anything: neither the sandals
of Aphra, so fast
    she covered a whole field of wheat
by running across the crests of the wheat-ears,
    nor everything Midas owned.
For people are not possessions.
    Lovers are not possessions,
neither each other's, nor their families'. If
    you have known love you should know that,
especially if you serve Artemis, whose brother
    told the truth. Cydippe's family
still lives, with many children, up at Iulis;
    their story came down to us in Zeno's collection,
the one with the islands' tales.

(*Galatea*, frag. 378)

ἢ μᾶλλον χρύσειον ἐν ὀφρύσιν ἱερὸν ἰχθύν

That island feast
    was more than a feast; there Kyra and Kassandra
met us, and there was golden-broiled giant bream with coriander,
    pounded with a mallet until tender,
green olives and capers and garlic and tiny lemons,
    and while I felt like a sleek finch on a sleek perch
while taking part in that repast,
    afterwards I just wanted to take a nap;
so we did, together,
    and when we woke it was dark, the moon scattered
her glitter all over the brine, and we were already
    entangled in each other, or rather
in one another,
    and so we decided to stay that way (letting Kassandra
take down her soft and complicated hair,
    and letting comfort alter
our positions as we chose, neither seeking
    nor finding much sleep),
and we stayed that way till the sun came up
    in the East.

7

(Lyric, frag. 227)

Ἔνεστ᾽ Ἀπόλλων τῷ χορῷ· τῆς λύρης ἀκούω·

Apollo has come to our house party, and Aphrodite,
    and also karaoke.
Whoever stays up till dawn
    goes home with the panettone,
or anything else left over, or anyone,
    provided he or she or they want to go home.
Castor and Pollux, send us company.
None of our friends deserves to sleep alone.

(Epigram 62)

Αἴνιε καὶ σὺ γὰρ ὧδε Μενέκρατες οὐκ ἐπὶ πουλὺ

Caro, you didn't seem to experience more
    than a little of our blowout last night.
What happened? Are you OK? You know I'm a friend you can trust.
    Honestly you look like someone decided to joust
against a centaur, or a champion equestrian,
    with your head as the grand prize.
Whom should I sue for excessive use of force?

"Calli, please
    let me go back to sleep upstairs if I can.
I don't know if it was the wine,
    or when I told Niko about my crush, thanks to that wine,
but I feel like I've been kicked in the nose by a horse."

9

(Epigram 64)

Οὕτως ὑπνώσαις, Κωνώπιον, ὡς ἐμὲ ποιεῖς

Sleep, Conopion, sleep
    as you make your admirer sleep
on the colder stones beside your bolted door;
sleep, Conopion, sleep
    without regrets, without a second thought
of the hardened and shivering man you don't want anymore.
If you wake, and stand, and see
    your lover prone under your window, and without
much hope of you to keep the chill away,
you'll surely go back to sleep
    and leave your neighbors to ask
what pitilessness could leave him there till day.

(*Aetia,* book 2, frag. 48)

ὥς τε Ζεὺς ἐράτιζε τριηκοσίους ἐνιαυτούς

Zeus (I read here) once made love for three hundred years.
It doesn't say how, or with whom.
Nor do we hear
whether his partner, or partners, were into it
that much, or one three-hundredth that much.
As for me, I'm just starved for touch,
or else exhausted from yearning every minute.
Unsatisfied love is a tomb.

(Epigram 43)

Εἰ μὲν ἑκών, Ἀρχῖν', ἐπεκώμασα, μυρία μέμφου,

It's easier to explain if we use Mr. Spock.
    Had it been my decision
to develop a crush on you, you may
       indeed have objected: it is most illogical.
It might, indeed, offend.
    And yet, if neurobiology will require
me to experience this emotion
       and, moreover, to communicate it, well . . .

    It's not like we can turn back the relevant clock;
it's not like I stood in your right-of-way
       at midnight and threw pebbles at your window.
All I did was leave a note on your door.
    I have been, and always shall be, your friend.

(Epigram 53)
Τὸν τὸ καλὸν μελανεῦντα Θεόκριτον, εἰ μὲν ἔμ' ἔχθει

The lord of the gods gets crushes on people too.
Theo has started to grow a lovely beard.
    If he's into me, may holy Zeus show him favor
in equal measure, as much as I love him—no,
      may Zeus favor him more,
          by a factor of four.

But if Theo won't text me back (so many guys
      make you wait, or ghost you), may Zeus despise
that beautiful man and everything he owns.
    May he be hated from now on. May he be feared.
May his heart weigh four times what it weighed before,
    so that he, too, feels this awkward,
        and has to stay home.

(*Hecale*, frag. 274)
ἁρμοῖ που κἀκείνῳ ἐπέτρεχε λεπτὸς ἴουλος

> Honestly I don't know
> if he'd want me to say so,
> but I love how he has just
> now started to grow a beard—
>
> I could tell from the delicate hair—no, the down
> on his cheek. I thought of the tips
> of the petals of the Italian immortelle
> which are, also, gold.
>
> I could see, when he blushed,
> his pride, his satisfaction
> (he had been waiting so long for it):
> he had just shaved.

(Epigram 32)

Θεσσαλικὲ Κλεόνικε, τάλαν, τάλαν, οὐ μὰ τὸν ὀξὺν

I hate to say it, Lee, but you look awful.
    I barely recognized you. Where have you been?
And you look so thin,

part sunburned, part pale as a bone.
    Now I get it. You've been hanging out
with Taylor, who has that effect on everyone.
    You look in their eyes and forget to eat,

    and then, after they forget
about you, nothing and no one else seems worthwhile,
    all other wishes canceled, all pleasure unlawful.

(Epigram 44)

Ἕλκος ἔχων ὁ ξεῖνος ἐλάνθανεν· ὡς ἀνιηρὸν

You were already in pain
when you came over for dinner, but the extent
of your internal injury didn't show
till that third glass of wine.
Then your face fell. It was like watching all the petals
drop from a rose at once—like time-lapse photography.
I couldn't not see it. I couldn't not see what it meant.
Someone broke into your heart and stole all the valuables.
I've been that kind of thief. But I didn't say so.
Instead I just said, "I've been there. I know."

(Epigram 45)
Ἔστι τι ναὶ τὸν Πᾶνα κεκρυμμένον, ἔστι τι ταύτῃ

Warm ashes may flare up when stirred,
no matter how gently. Hermes, Dionysus, and Pan—
god of ferment, god of wild woods, god of pretenders—
created me that way; maybe I ought to feel shame,
and yet, to tell the truth, I'd rather not skip it.

That said, I hope he won't rush me.
            You might have heard.
That quiet one who tilts his head like a whippet
has only to touch me,
and I fall apart like a heap of cinders.
An underground stream can topple a granite home.

(*Hecale*, frag. 256)
λέξομαι ἐν μυχάτῳ· κλισίη δέ μοί ἐστιν ἑτοίμη

Don't worry, you
    can have the bed; I'll take the couch
by the door, in the living room, as usual.

(Iamb 10, frag. 200a)

Τὰς Ἀφροδίτας—ἡ θεὸς γὰρ οὐ μία—

There are so many versions of Aphrodite,
so many incarnations.
The one I first met in the Castro beats all the rest,
for wisdom, I mean. For wisdom.
She, and she only, accepts sacrifices of pork.
She is the goddess of no particular nation,
no singular standard of beauty,
no rules at the door. No one form of love is best.
Michel did a lot to support her: I thank him
for that, though otherwise he was a jerk.

(Epigram 27)

Ὤμοσε Καλλίγνωτος Ἰωνίδι μήποτ᾽ ἐκείνης

Once they decided to make a home together
    Cal told Ione that he would never consider
anybody else as his regular lover;
    all of us knew he was bi, but he said he would never
place any guy, or any woman, above her.
    Now it's as if he were poisoned, or else on fire,
throwing off sparks left and right, for a brand-new crush,
    who happens to be nonbinary. As for
Ione, all his friends now have to push
    ourselves to see, or even to think about her,
poor girl, who last week thought she was his primary.

(Epigram 24)

Ἀστακίδην τὸν Κρῆτα τὸν αἰπόλον ἥρπασε Νύμφη

The shepherds I know tell stories for one another,
   and mostly they're not about Daphne escaping Apollo,
      dramatic natural disasters,
or even the broad sails of the bravest Argives.
   We prefer Scott and Emma, or Gray and Tess,
      who crossed a continent to be together,
having realized that each would follow
      the other anywhere, that they would rather
rip up their lives than stay apart, that their loves
were real and true and strong,
   no less so for how long
      they themselves believed they were more like sisters, or
      brothers.

(Epigram 33)

Ὠγρευτής, Ἐπίκυδες, ἐν οὔρεσι πάντα λαγωὸν

When you can't be with somebody you want to be with—
    you're too far away, or it's not allowed—
your love for them takes on the status of myth.
    When you're always together, it's harder.

In the same way, the dedicated hunter
    tracks the fugitive deer or rabbit through mist,
bramble, frost,
    mud, snow, rotten ice, and swamp water
before day's blinding glare or night's thick shroud.
    Yet bring the same
hunter the same prey animal, tamed,
    or wounded, or docile, or otherwise ready for slaughter,
and the hunter will decide—
               Um, no.
    Love shouldn't work like that. If love is a hunt,
it should be about who you want
    at your back, or by your side
with dagger, chakram, trident, or short bow,
    not what you string up in your larder.

(Epigram 39)

Τὰ δῶρα τἀφροδίτῃ

It's hard work making people fall in love,
      even harder to get them to stay that way. No wonder
my friend Simone has built, for the goddess of love,
      an idiosyncratic altar:
on it, one tube of lip gloss, a charm bracelet, car keys,
      a rental agreement for a basement apartment,
a doorbell, a star for a Christmas tree, a salt or
      pepper shaker, the mouthpiece
for a pocket trumpet, a pill splitter, and under
      them all, a folded velvet satchel,
in which the lucky couple
      who stay together into a shared old age
can keep whatever other sentiment-
      al objects they decide to save.

(*Aetia*, book 4, frag. 101a)

Ἥρῃ τῇ Σαμίῃ περὶ μὲν τρίχας ἄμπελος ἕρπει

Snakes stand for danger, but also for things intertwining,
    pairs of sacred opposites:
companionship and time alone,
    or sun and fog, or jealousy and compersion.
Thus the snake-shaped grape-
    vine, with its bits
and buds, its shining
    granite scales, that a master carver set
in low relief around the combed-out locks
    of Hera in the lovely stone
        of the Samian idol, its style
    Eastern, almost Persian,
is not, as some assume, a spiteful crown
    reflecting her victory over Dionysus,
her husband's son who is not her son,
    but rather a hopeful sign
        of what's now on her mind:
    this version of Hera finds
great joy in the knowledge
    of lovers intertwined,
as long as they're equals, as long as they're enthusiastic.
    To bloom and grow in more than one
        direction, like the garland, is a privilege,
        though also an exertion.
        It's fantastic,
    as long as it's not a pursuit or a power play:
as long as it's warm rain on a bright day,
    not a thunderclap, or an atmospheric inversion.

(*Aetia,* book 4, frag. 101b)

Ἥρη τῇ Σαμίῃ περὶ μὲν τρίχας ἄμπελος ἕρπει

Snakes stand for danger, but also for things intertwining,
    pairs of sacred opposites:
companionship and time alone,
    or sun and fog, or jealousy and compersion.
Apollo once had trouble sharing them
    with other gods, since snakes were his own emblem;
you might not have seen him as one of the quiet divinities,
    much less
as a patron of introverts and introversion,
    but all the arts (so he used to believe) are his,
and in his youth he spent too much time pining
    for girls who would rather be trees.
Yet in the version
    of his life that I prefer,
        he's far
from bossy: he shows affinities
    for lyricists and sculptors and portrait
painters who work best at dusk and dawn,
    who draw with ash and earth, with charcoal, crayon
        or pale
    inkstones; whose art consists
of undertone and trill, hint and subversion,
    without a single lead. It's an ensemble
cast, whose hits
    are trios and duets,
sometimes in third, sometimes in second person.

(Epigram 47)

Ὡς ἀγαθὰν Πολύφαμος ἀνεύρετο τὰν ἐπαοιδὰν

Fun fact: long ago, in the age of myth
    (so Theocritus says) Polyphemus the Cyclops discovered
a remedy for the pains of unsatisfied lovers;
    pursued by the vision of someone he'd never be with,
he lifted his lyre and made up a song about it.
The Muses know what they're doing. He was wise.

Such wisdom cures all aches.
    In the same way, starvation
removes the dissatisfaction
    of longing; it's quite a cure for that disease,
and surely we ought to know how to defend

ourselves. Erotic love is merciless,
    but you and I, Polyphemus, can live without it.
We're not afraid of you, Love. We know many ways
    to pin your wings.
I have one friend
    who cuts herself. I know another who sings.

2

(Epigram 8)

Στήλην μητρυιῆς, μικρὰν λίθον, ἔστεφε κοῦρος

The fuckers renamed an airport for a tyrant
    who wouldn't stop lying, and couldn't stand people like me,
and rarely flew commercial while he lived.
    "Why do you have to keep dragging him? Can't you forgive
the dead?" Well, no.
    Every time I go home there's a monument
to a man whose culpable indifference
    sent my peers to their early graves,
a glib smiler, a bad dad who deserves infamy.
    It seems like something people today should know.

(*Hecale*, frag. 275)
πάσχομεν ἄστηνοι· τὰ μὲν οἴκοθε πάντα δέδασται

It hurts to be poor. It hurts more,
   these days, when any agent of the crown
can come to our houses and take anything we own
   for his own use,
and then send us to jail.
   They call it security, or a lien, or bail.
but we have come to believe their ample store
   of names are simply names for the same ruse.

(frag. 556, 638, 644)

νυμφίε Δημοφόων, ἄδικε ξένε
ἵλαθί μοι φαλαρῖτι, πυλαιμάχε
νόμον δ᾽ ἤειδεν Ἄρηος

Choose me, Athena, defender
    of crafts and order,
and of the just
    city-state,
where no one gets lost;

let me be chosen
    in the next election,
even if the ballot
    counters have to
stay up late.

Let as many
    citizens cast
well-considered votes
    as poets have called your helmet
"brightly-embossed." Let

my voice be
    your conduit; a god such as
yourself is equal
    to any task, if it please
you to take action.

My opponent can sing, but he
    sings and prays
to Ares,
    who picks fights with guests;
who glories in injuries

and cruelties,
    in strife and spoils, in the wasteful
burning of oil,
    in domination
and faction.

31

(frag. 388)

Φωκαέων μέχρις κε φανῇ μέγας εἰν ἁλὶ μύδρος

> Berenice, rightful governor
>> who looks out for our town, we will stay
> at your side, and by your side,
>> and on your side,
>
>> till the famous hot ingots the size
> and weight of a steer,
>> which the Phoceans dumped in their harbor
>
> to impede a hostile navy, reappear,
>> floating, at high tide;
> till every attendant truly wants
>> to attend the fancy-dress ball;
>
>> till Pallas Athena tells us all
> she's pregnant, and Artemis
>> ends up as some dude's bride.

(Aetia, book 2, frag. 44–51)

Αἴγυπτος προπάροιθεν ἐπ᾽ ἐννέα κάρφετο ποίας

All the Greek cities have seen their refugees;
    only one has shown them pity,
let alone hospitality.
    Most of the rest look back to the practice
of Phalaris, who roasted
    dark-skinned foreigners alive
inside an enormous bull,
    believing it would bring his kingdom
luck, or prevent drought.

    I know whom I think Zeus loves,
and whom I'd like to see kicked out.

(*Aetia*, book 4, frag. 90)

Ἔνθ᾿, Ἄβδηρ᾿, οὗ νῦν [. . . .]λεω φαρμακὸν ἀγινεῖ

The way a word like sanction, or inflammable,
    and its opposite are the same,
our town feels like two towns, or maybe three:
    one where we welcome
strangers, where they feel able
    to call it home,
and one where we throw the foreigners into the sea.

(*Aetia*, book 4, frag. 104)

Οἰσύδρεω Θρήϊκος ἐφ᾽ αἵματι πολλὰ Θάσοιο

Dear Thracians—no, dear citizens
    of Thrace: you've got blood on your hands.
Sooner or later justice, or vengeance, or
    something, will take care
of you, just as you took care
    of the people who used to live
on what you call your lands.

(*Aetia*, book 3, frag. 64)

Οὐδ᾽ ἄν τοι Καμάρινα τόσον κακὸν ὁκκόσον ἀνδρός

You're the kind of rich dude who drains wetlands
    to put in high-end one-bedrooms,
so it's no surprise you plan to demolish
    a holy tomb.
Take it from me, though: don't. I am Simonides,
    and I've been dead for a while.
The reverent Acragians put up
    a mausoleum for me, dedicated to Zeus,
defender of migrants; Governor Fenix—
    he's infamous now—tore it down
in order to build a tower he named for himself.
    Later he prayed for forgiveness. No use.

(*Aetia*, book 3, frag. 84–85)

Ἦλθες ὅτ᾽ ἐκ Πίσης, Εὐθύκλεες, ἄνδρας ἐλέγξας

People are going to hate you once you've won.
    You're going to come home from the contest, the biggest game,
bringing your shared reward: four teams of mules,
    which you selected, out there near the capital,
so farmers around here would have an easier time,
        You took their household needs to heart.
    But when you get home, those farmers are going to listen
to the spineless ones, the spreaders of slander
    who also count votes,
who say it's all a trap, that you take bribes,
    that you can't be trusted, having learned
the language of the coast, and eaten odd fruit.
    They will cast their ballots against you,
smash your ceramics, melt your bronze gods down,
    break your kitchen table up for logs.
        And later they'll learn. They'll learn.
Soon enough there will be another election,
    and then the takers of bribes will be shown the door,
or possibly fed to the dogs.

(Hymn 1: To Zeus)

Now we pour out wine
    to honor Zeus, lord
of other lords, who drove
    the Titans away, and came to determine
justice for humans on earth, and for other gods.
    (I say what things should be,
as they must be if you rule all,
    and not as they appear to us on Earth.)

    But what to sing, and how? Where
to begin? Where was he born?
    There is a Cretan mountain, and another
in Arcadia, with your tombs.
    Which one is lying? A famous Cretan
said, "All Cretans are liars." But, lord,
    they both lie; anyone lies
who says you have a tomb, though the Cretans
    built one for you, full of ornament
(that sort of shrine, designed
    with pilgrims' coin in mind,
might as well be a tomb).
    You do not die. You are always and everywhere.

    But you were born: in Arcadia.
Your mother Rhea bore you in a thicket.
    After she, that gentle titan,
placed you for the first time on her skin,
    she started to look for fresh water,
to wash out the blood, to swathe the dirt away.
    But running water
didn't exist. Not even in Arcadia.
    Those sites that tourists visit
for their rivers? Not yet.
    Not back then.
When Rhea brought
    your body from inside hers, into the air,
the rivers Ion and Mela
    might have been flat dirt roads,

and Carno, which floods so often—
    snakes struggled, back then, for the privilege
of carving out dry burrows there.

Rhea was at a loss.
    She said to the lovely dirt,
"As I have given birth,
    so you give birth: let there be running water
for gods, and for human beings."
    She lifted her rosy-brown arm and whacked
the mountain itself with her scepter.
    And the mountain opened up,
and there were springs, and pools,
    and rills and waterfalls, and fluent streams,
and rivers and lakes and bathing spots and shrines,
    the kind where we now wash ourselves, and bless
the birth of Zeus. And she scrubbed
    your powerful tiny body, and brought you to Nidia,
your first nurse,
    who cared for you and hid you when your father
sought you (to eat you),
    and that is why we call the river that gives
fresh water to the towns
    of the Caucasus the Nidian River,
the oldest river for the oldest towns.

    Nidia brought you to Crete,
first to what was already the mountain Thena,
    and then to what is now the capital, Knossos.
The first Cretans, Lord, the first Cretans
    who deserve to live
in human memory
    devoted themselves to you:
Melia, and Adrasti who gave you
    a nap in a golden bed
(golden with soft wet leaves, of course, since linen
    had not been invented)
and then took your still-tiny divine body
    to the goat Amalthea,
so you could drink her fatty milk.
    She was a holy goat.

And suddenly then for the first time
　　bees made honey; for you knew
you needed, and therefore created,
　　the honeycomb, made by bees,
so you could taste its sugars.
　　Meanwhile those low divinities
whose name sounds much like "Charities"
　　performed a kind of concussive percussion dance,
picking the parts of their armor apart
　　to bang on them, and binding them
together so they would clang—they were the first cymbals.
　　That way Kronos, your father and would-be
murderer, would not hear your baby cries.

　　Lord of the Heavens, you grew.
Lord of the Heavens, you
　　could nourish yourself;
you were a youth, not a child,
　　your cheek no longer smooth.
That's when your elders decided
　　that you should live in Heaven.
Old poets got this part wrong.
　　You in the heavens and ruling the Earth,
Poseidon for the ocean, Hades
　　for the dead—supposedly
you and your brothers drew lots.
　　But you and your brothers aren't idiots.
Why would any god
　　agree to a game of chance,
when one of the chances is Heaven?

No, those poets were wrong.
　　You became the god
who rules over all the gods
　　because your early deeds
determined that you could;
　　that you could weave the lightning,
rip through the clouds, and see the entire Earth.
　　Of course the most magnificent
of all the raptors would become your sign,
　　whose feathers shake and rearrange the wind;

Of course the particular skill
　　you sponsor among human beings
is the hardest of all:
　　not for you navigation, not for you
the phalanx,
　　not for you the lyre,
much less the syrinx.
　　You rule over the rulers,
you give the laws to the lawmakers.
　　No human being, we say, is above the law.
Bronzesmiths and blacksmiths pray to their Hephaestus,
　　archers to Artemis; singers to her bright twin.
But you are the patron of those
　　who hold a public trust,
who hold appointive office, or win elections.
　　Kings remain kings when you say so.
(I say what things should be,
　　as they must be if you rule all,
and not as they appear to us on Earth.)
　　All have their eyes on you, and you on them.
You see the kleptocrat, and the autocrat,
　　and the habitual liar, and the officials
who neither consult, nor seek consent.
　　You are stronger than they are; you overrule.

　　Son of Kronos, who overthrew Kronos,
protector of protectors,
　　the giver of laws for those who give laws
and receive them,
　　the guarantor of public harmony
of citizens' and migrants' physical safety,
　　without which other virtues fall apart,
lord, guard our choice of rulers,
　　and every ruler's choice,
from town council seats to the whole Alexandrian shore.
　　"Political action in its source is pure,
but in its civil function" needs protection,
　　and you are the protector of protectors,
father of charity, maker of comfort and wealth,
　　of fairness and justice and mercy.

(I say what things should be,
    as they must be if you rule all,
and not as they appear to us on Earth.)
    Without virtue no one is safe,
without prosperity, nobody is secure.
    We pray for those things, high god of all the other gods,
here at your windy precipice, whose edge
    and altar welcome the golden eagle,
in honor of you, Zeus, for whom
    we now pour out the wine.

3

(*Aetia*, book 1, frag. 31g, and frag. 620 and 731)
Τὼ]ς μὲν ἔφη· τὰς δ᾽ εἶθαρ ἐμὸς πάλιν εἴρετο θυμός
ἄγνωτον μηδὲν ἔχοιμι καλόν
τὴν θεῦν Ἄρτεμιν οἳ ᾽ ἔπαθεν

What the—
   why does this statue of Artemis, whom I revere,
have a clove of garlic tied to her left ear,
   and why do the temple tenders place a shallow
mortar, for garlic, over her fine short hair?
   Does this sort of thing have any basis in myth?

It does—I keep back nothing for reasons of tact,
   nothing that I consider beautiful;
the goddess herself once chose this crown, or halo,
   When the Epirians attacked
this town, they tried to mock, desecrate, and defile
   her manless status
by smearing her head with garlic.
   The idea
was that she had not truly rejected marriage
but rather stank so bad no man could want her.
   (What girl hasn't heard, and heard again,
that if we work too hard, no man will date us?)

The citizens drove the Epirians into the sea.
Pounded raw garlic means a campfire, a meal for
   a hunter, and for the friends of a hunter.
The goddess has never cared to pair off with men,
   not now, and not in any former age,
but the regional cuisine
   now emphasizes garlic and *faskomilo*,
also known as sage.

(*Aetia*, book 3, frag. 79)

Τεῦ δὲ χάριν . . . κικλήσ]κουσιν

There are so many—too many,
    say men who know nothing about it—divinities
who have given birth.
    So why
do those among us who struggle with balky wombs,
    with not-yet-
visible infants inside us that tumble and roll,
    and yaw and pitch and cancel each night's sleep,
why do we pray
    so often to Artemis,
who runs barefoot and never loved a man?

Because she never loved a man, some say.
Others say: just because she is fleet of foot,
    and figures out how to travel without delay.
Hers is the night hunt, the goddess who finds the way.
    I think there is another reason, though.
I think she is the only god or goddess
    on the entire mountain of Olympia
or over or under or within sight of it
    who neither gives orders to other divinities,
nor ever tried, much less agreed, to obey.

(*Aetia*, book 3, frag. 65)

Αὐτομά[της . . .] εὐναὲς ἐπών[υμον, ἀλ]λ᾽ ἀπὸ σ[εῖ]ο

Nobody wants to talk about lochia. Or about menstruation.
But really we should.
The lovely and ample fountain in Argos named Purity
belongs to the city; domestic workers clean
themselves there, so men say the appellation
must be a long-running joke. Those men are mean
and should not hold positions of authority.
The fountain and its purpose are pure and good.

(Lyric, frag. 226)

Ἡ Λῆμνος τὸ παλαιόν, εἴ τις ἄλλη

Pour one out for women who date men.
    Such women are instructed to remain
at all times beautiful, yet approachable,
    lips marked with beeswax, brows
faintly brushed with charcoal,
    and never to come off as powerful,
on pain of abandonment.

    There are other choices. For example.
Legends call Lemnos the Island
    of No Husbands, because
(supposedly) all husbands there took lovers,
    after which their first wives murdered them.

That's not what happened. The women had cause.
    Their husbands sailed away and made new lives,
and as for the now ex-wives,
    my goddess Artemis made them a promise:

having once tried to follow the well-worn pattern,
    having been labeled prudes
when they refused, and slatterns
    when they said yes, and having been celebrated
for carrying a child
    until the time arrived for them to deliver,
they ceased their hymns and libations
    to Aphrodite, and shifted their patronage

to my own silver goddess, who gave
    them the way of the bow-
string and quiver,
    and warranted, when they asked
about their duties in marriage—
    not only in bed, but in the connubial kitchen,
where they used to listen
    to men, defer to men's tasks, and wrap lunches for men—
that nothing like that would happen to them again.

(*Aetia*, book 3, frag. 80–82)

αἰδοῖ δ᾽ ὡς φοί[νικι] τεὰς ἐρύθουσα παρειάς

Remember when we didn't get along?
    And now you blush, telling your story—
which isn't all mine to tell—while you squeeze my hand.
    I can, however, share an allegory,
or maybe more of a long-ago parallel.
    Myus and Milesia—which are cities,
not people—were at war. For decades.
    Stupidly at war. No one knew how to end it
without sacrificing some potentate's dignity.
    No one could safely or legally cross the border,
except at one shrine that, according to ancient treaty,
    had to welcome citizens of both
to the festival for Artemis.
    Her temple columns glistened, as if
to soften and oil the world, saying "All
    worshippers are welcome; no sword
on shield will mar this space, and no spears thrown,
    no horses whipped to frenzy or retreat.
Would it were thus in forest and field."
                                    She loved
    to see this temple as her gathering place,
where prayers rose only to her. But it was hard
    for women from Myus to get there.
They could claim safe passage. But they were exhausted
    from passing through war zones. They arrived afraid.
So after many a season of hints and omens
    and disregarded divinations, fletchings,
and bronze spear tips interpreted
    across the temple floor,
the goddess reached out
    to that other goddess from Cyprus,
the one who was born out of foam,
    and challenged her to prove that she—
having started a war—could stop one,
    that she, the Cyprian, was a diplomat
to excel all diplomats, that she could inspire
    oratory enough, not just

49

to make people disrobe,
    but to make them disarm.
The next two
    adult women in the temple,
the planners of next year's procession, were Katia,
    granddaughter of Cydippe, from Milesia,
and Yana from Myus. They came
    holding maps, only slowly meeting each other's gaze,
protected by winter blankets that doubled as cloaks,
    so they could spend the night on that cold floor,
and wary of the mission, wondering if
    they could even get home
unharmed . . . they removed their thick boots . . .
    they began to talk about swords, and parades,
about the sources for the purest spring,
    about how to dress
a fresh-killed deer and craft a glove
    out of deer velvet. their hands
as models . . . their wrists . . . about how to make
    the best cloak (trying out
each drape and each trace on each other) . . .

Since that day the two of them
have lived inseparable.
    Even their names fit together: Katyana.
Myus and Milesia are at peace,
    as if they were one home,
and Artemis, lovely, fierce Artemis,
    whose shadow is sleek at twilight, gone
at sunrise, knows
    she need not act alone.

(Epigram 54)

Καὶ πάλιν, Εἰλήθυια, Λυκαινίδος ἐλθὲ καλεύσης

Goddess of parturition, listen when Cleo
calls. Accept her offerings and her fears
before the hardest task,
and make it as easy as it can ever
be for her to give birth.
                    "Do you know whether
you're having a girl or boy?" Sweet clue-
less grownup, the only way is to ask
the child. We're not going to know for years.

(Epigram 55)

Τὸ χρέος ὡς ἀπέχεις, Ἀσκληπιέ, τὸ πρὸ γυναικὸς

Asclepius, god of medicine, we've paid
   your bill. Andrea's wife
has safely given birth: you protected her life.
   I have carved, in stone, this record of our deal
so nobody (least of all you, my lord) can say
   it will not last, or was not real.

(Epigram 35)

Ἄρτεμι, τὶν τόδ᾽ ἄγαλμα Φιληρατὶς εἴσατο τῆδε·

Artemis! Phileratis has placed
    this image here in your honor.
Let her work, and yours in protecting her, not go to waste;
    may you, with your sandals and bow, look kindly upon her.

(Iambs, frag. 223)

κοὐχ ὧδ᾽ Ἀρίων τὠπέσαντι πὰρ Διί

Horses don't get periods. They used to.
    Mares, fertile cats, cattle, ferrets—all used to bleed
a lot, as many of us still do.

    Then the mare Arion,
the daughter of Demeter and Poseidon,
    had to cross the known world as fast as possible
to save her own child from a kidnapper, a Titan.
    The land she had to cross was arable
until she crossed it, hooves packing the moist spring soil
    into dry pebbles with her weight and speed.
She slept upright in Zeus's Nemean shrine.
    Then her monthly cycle came. She could not travel
till it passed.
    Her knees and hindquarters and eyelids blazed with pain.
    She prayed to her father and mother to spare her and hers,
and they agreed,
    on behalf of all four-footed creatures, every steed,
pasture creature, ungulate, canine
    and feline,
that this month's cycle would be their last.

(Epigram 51)

Τὴν Φρυγίην Αἴσχρην, ἀγαθὸν γάλα, πᾶσιν ἐν ἐσθλοῖς

Child-care workers deserve to retire with pensions.
Micah—who's rich— made sure the woman who gave
him his bottle could save
her late years for travel, or rest; then, to draw attention
(he liked to explain) to people in her situation
he put up this statue. It's hard to overlook.
He said it was even better than writing a book.

(Iambs, frag. 223)

κοὐχ ὦδ᾽ Ἀρίων τὠπέσαντι πὰρ Διί

As in *Hamlet*, but harmless,
I put the ear-infection medicine drop
    by drop into my baby's ear.
Then my baby awoke. The horses of Poseidon
    did not thrash so hard,
nor did the god of the sea feel half so helpless,
    nearly choked with pointless fear.

Then, as if she had
    been trying to decide on
a logical stopping point, she sat up,
    and the tears came to a full stop,
thanks be to Zeus. May she never again feel so sad.

(*Aetia*, book 1, frag. 27)

ἄρνες τοι, φίλε κοῦρε, συνήλικες, ἄρνες ἑταῖροι

    You were always a lamb,
soft child; you played among
    lambs, and slept with the lambs
in their fold,
    as if you knew or believed that you
were not,
    that you could never be, too old.

(*Hecale*, frag. 271)
σὺν δ᾽ ἡμῖν ὁ πελαργὸς ἀμορβεύεσκεν ἀλοίτης

Why is the stork called an avenger?
    Middle schoolers send her messages:
You owe me for bringing me here.
    And so she torments their abusers,
pecking at them, dropping turds in their Mountain Dews
    from very high up, and snatching or
scratching their jackets, gloves, scarves, sunglasses
    and caps, year after unrelenting year.

(Iambs, frag. 221)

αἰτοῦμεν εὐμάθειαν Ἑρμᾶνος δόσιν

In my poems about the origins of things
    I forgot to include the most important thing
if you've got a school-age child: how to get
    your child out of bed first thing
        in the morning.

The answer seems
to be: first, get enough rest
    yourself; then pray to Hermes, god of memes
and pranks and D&D and shaggy-dog stories, that he will let
    the school provide one thing
the kids will consider their thing,
    and not the teachers' thing.
        Freedom, or at least
the illusion of freedom, works better than any warning.

(Epigram 35)

Ἄρτεμι, τὶν τόδ᾽ ἄγαλμα Φιληρατὶς εἵσατο τῆδε·

This morning Patricia drew her own picture
    of Artemis.
Each arrow has clean-
    feathered fletching,
each sandal its buckle of leather
    and fine bone.

Acknowledge the picture and keep her
    safe, proud goddess,
and let her do well; she's worried
    about her biology test.
She thinks she can't pass
    on her own.

(Epigram 41)

Ἱερέη Δήμητρος ἐγώ ποτε καὶ πάλιν Καβείρων

"My daughter won't leave her room, even though
    she's old enough to date;
her grandmother says she'll be an old maid.
    Also she keeps her door locked." And no wonder.

Not only did she get to know
    her genuine friends online; she's tired
or more than tired, of what she's heard
    from you every day since eighth grade

about foundation and blush and toner and other
    components of an attractive face,
which she might not even want. Please give her space.

    Don't assume anything is a phase she'll get over,
or (worse) outgrow; ask what she wants. Promise to hear.
    That said, she might not tell you—directly—ever,
or not for donkey's years.

(*Hecale*, frag. 248)

γεργέριμον πίτυρίν τε καὶ ἣν ἀπεθήκατο λευκήν

I wish you wouldn't yell at me for trying.
  Brown olives should be picked before they are ripe;
pale olives are good for lamb stew, but must be pitted,
    then stored in brine.
People are different, too. When the bitter
    black olive, determined to keep
      its shape, insists
it shouldn't be crushed with the green ones,
    good cooks know it isn't malingering, or lying.

(*Aetia,* book 4, frag. 97)

Τυρσηνῶν τείχισμα Πελασγικὸν εἶχέ με γαῖα

Sometimes you just hit a wall.
    Me, for example. I am one of the walls
the tribal people who lived here built
    of earth and dirt and stones. Or maybe the gods
made me. I mark the city's outer bounds.
    I say: you can build and adjust
and lead your children up to a certain point,
    no more. It would be unjust
as well as impractical, or impossible,
    to train them in better behavior: they will ignore you;
you may call them home and they will not care;
    they will run away fast; they will treat you as if your mouth
could make no sound,
    or communicate with you only in parables;
they will go as far as they must,
    no, as far as they think they must, to find
something like their own unsettled ground.

(Hymn 3: To Artemis)

What does Artemis want with attention? Of all the gods
    she takes the least from human beings:
for part of the year, she wants to be left alone.
    She has not changed,
since the day she asked her father:
"Let me stay a girl; let me never marry.
    Let me take many names, so my brother
will never be jealous of one.
    And give me a quiver—no, don't;
the Cyclopes can do that,
    But give me the power to allot moonlight,
and let me wear a tunic cut no lower
    than the knee, with a smooth woven edge,
so my dress won't slow me down.
    Give me companions
my own age, daughters of Ocean
    whom nobody will bother about marriage,
and give me assistants, river goddesses
    to clean my running shoes and patch my boots,
Let me rule every free mountain,
    and as for all these cities built by men,
I'll visit them when pregnant women need me."

She said, and kept trying to reach her tiny hand
    high up, to touch the hairs in the beard
of Zeus, who laughed and nodded; he agreed.
    "A daughter like you," said Zeus,
"is worth the anger of Hera. What you ask
    I grant. Your father will give you greater things too.
I'll give you thirty cities,
    each with its tower, that call no other god theirs."
(The girl goddess shrugged.) "And there will be cities you share
    with other gods, sea-island city-states
and cities in the middle of great plains,
    and you will be called
Defender of Harbors and Ways." And he nodded,
    satisfied. And then she ran away,
the girl god who loved running, into the woods
    of Crete, over its white mountain,

and then to the shore, to find other girls
    like her. And she found many,
none of whom wanted to dress up, none of whom wanted
    to grow into womanhood, whatever that means,
or seek a man's hand, ever. Some of the girls
    were daughters of like-minded rivers; the river Caratos, for
        instance,
so that the river itself ran and laughed and was glad.

    Then she sought the smithies of the Cyclopes.
She found them on their island, by their anvils,
    the ones Hephaestus made from meteorites,
tending their ingots, making something amazing:
    drinking troughs for the whitecaps, also called
the horses of Poseidon. All of her companion
    girls stood paralyzed by fear,
beholding the mountainous Cyclopes, each one's eye
    the size of a hoplite's shield,
some of them yelling,
    lifting and swinging the massive spikes and mallets
with which they hit their anvils. It was awful,
    or rather awe-inspiring: Mount Aetna
exclaimed in sympathetic pain, and heavy Trinax,
    and the whole Italian peninsula.
It scared the girls, who—being daughters of Ocean—
    had special reason to be scared:
when one of the Ocean girls breaks a household rule,
    her mother says some Cyclops will come get her,
then Hermes shows up, in his hand a big stick on fire,
    ash on his forehead making a unibrow,
and of course the girl
    shocked witless, runs into her mother's arms.

    Artemis herself is harder to scare.
When you were a toddler, my goddess,
    Leto came here with you, and handed you
to Hephaestus, so he would promise a dowry,
    yours when you should wed.
She held out your body to him, but you heard his promise,
    including the word that means wedding, and ripped out his hair.
That's why the god of the bellows, to this day
    has a receding hairline,

65

with a smooth spot up top.
    It's also why the din his employees
raise struck you, this time, as NBD.

"Cyclopes," you said, "I'll need a recurve bow,
    and arrows, and hoops for a quiver.
You made them for Apollo; make them for me!
    In return: when I track and kill
a meaty monster, an enormous beast—
    and you know I will—you get the flanks,
the thighs, or the top sirloin—your choice—to eat."
    Of course they did exactly as you asked.
Faster than any human being could
    you slung that bow over your shoulder, and that quiver
over your back, and ran to Arcadia
    to fetch puppies (yes, of course you get puppies)
from wild Pan. You found him ripping slices
    of raw meat from a dead lynx
to feed them full. And after the puppies had supper
    he gave them to you: two half black and half white,
like cookies, called Sobel and Sabel; three more,
    each ruddy and eager, and one
with almond patches and alert black ears,
    whose fur, on a cat, you might call calico.
They were the kind of pups who could drag lions
    by the skin,
living lions, I mean. And he gave you seven
    adult dogs, each one able to breed and give birth—
our word "cynosure" comes from them,
    meaning the best dogs, the ones who can catch anything.

On the way out of the woods you discovered deer,
    a great lot of them. Your dogs brought down
four out of five, unharmed,
    so that you could collar and drive them,
and train them to pull your cart.
    One deer escaped by crossing the vast Blue River,
the deer that was Heracles's prize during his labors,
    Heracles who has been known
to hang out in front of the mansion of the gods,
    hoping you'll bring something fat and thick

and freshly killed for him to roast
   or grill. He says to you, when you get back to Olympus,
"Why don't you just shoot the most dangerous beasts?
   Then you'd have more worshippers,
like me. Why bother hare or deer?
   They've never hurt a mortal. But these wild boars—
they trample grain and grapes, crush trenches, crash
   through half-built wooden houses.
Also wild bulls are very bad and dangerous.
   I think you should only shoot those."
Then he turned back to butcher the hairy boar,
   his favorite fatty meal.

Artemis! you are the god of the silver moon,
   and yet you shine like gold, you are a god
of girls, your body is her own,
   your arms and belt and arrows are your own,
your deer are all your own, with shining bridles.
What peaks and groves and coverts
   are your favorites?
(Is that like asking who is your best friend?)
   Your island Dolix, your city Perigee,
your hill Taege, your harbor Eurypos:
   these are among your favorites,
and not the only ones.
   As for your best friend,
or first, or closest, friend,
   you love the girl called Britomart, or Gwent—
her bow never misses. I think
   you laid a spell on it,
though maybe it's just practice. She's also
   the girl in that story about lovesick King Minos,
who thrashed himself and roamed the hills of Crete,
   basically stalking her. For a long time she hid.
She hid every day among scrubby water oaks
   or laid low in river meadows
so he would overlook her. This kind of thing
   continued for nine months.
(Crete has a problem with stalkers. It starts at the top.)
   This king looked underground, and hacked through trees

whose hollows (he thought) could hide a nymph,
   and would not stop for anything, until
he caught her beside a cliff, a witness, a martyr—
   so he believed—to his own sick version of love.
She knew what to do. She leapt right into the sea,
   into the web the fishers of Coëins
(one of Crete's five provinces) maintain,
   and the recoil from the nets' cords did not kill her,
but drenched her in salt, and strong as spider-silk,
   it broke her fall. They call her Spider-Gwent,
after her spiderlike save;
   the pool she fell into became, in her honor, Gwent-pool.
She loves you, and she likes her independence;
   she doesn't want to be your only girl.
You also go out with Karen; you gave her dogs,
   the dogs your friend Hepzibah trained
to win cart-races. And you've been seen beside Keif,
   whose curly hair pops and glows
against her ebony skin; she married Kalfa,
   and also runs with you.
As for Antiklea,
   you love her as you love moonlight,
and sightlines, and speed, and air, and your own clear eyes.
   These girls became the first to roam
the Earth with speedy arrows, in a pack,
   to carry over one shoulder the quiver and bow.
Shrines honor them because they honor you.

At the Ephesian seaside
   the Amazons placed your idol,
bow at the ready, with stone carved like your hounds,
   two courant, one rampant, one salient,
before them the ocean, behind them a broad oak tree.
   Hippolyta, the Amazons' first queen,
created a holy rite:
   they dance in their armor, as men do in Athens, and then
they stand in a circle and one of them plays the horn,
   so loud the arrows in their quivers shake.
That shrine still stands,
   with sturdier walls around it. I have seen it.
Nothing is brighter at dawn, nor in the full moon.

How and where and how often did you practice—
    not that you needed practice;
all humans do; you are a god—
    how did you start to practice
firing your bow?
    Once at an elm, and an oak, and a fugitive boar,
and then
    at the windows of houses of unjust men,
thieves and bullies, the kind
    who turn away refugees.
Even today you punish their pride. Back then
    you gave their cattle blackleg and grimy pneumonia,
and turned their grain stores thin
    and white, like old men's hair,
and made their own hair fall out.
    Some of them—for you denied them
the dignity they denied others—spent
    the rest of their lives with a literal pain in the ass.

    But the first generation
to admit mistakes, to roast and bake and offer
    to feast the stranger—
they and their households
    were never without: the furrows they dug
bore corn; whatever they raised that went on four legs
    lived to adulthood and flourished.
Moreover, Artemis, goddess, you reward
    practice, and virtue, and intense attention,
the kind of intensity that tries
    to break its own records, rather than shove others down.
Your fans are not mean girls; no one is mired in the discourse;
    your households never split; they accept in-laws,
and nobody has to separate friends from friends.
    Let me sit among those friends myself,
or rather stand with them, Artemis, in your honor,
    outdoors and in, rain or shine, giving banquets or kudos,
making and never forgetting your worthiest song.

4

(Epigram 42)

Ἥμισύ μευ ψυχῆς ἔτι τὸ πνέον, ἥμισυ δ᾽ οὐκ οἶδ᾽

Half of me—an intangible half—is alive;
    the other part has gone I don't know where—
either it's dead, or it's lost in what it calls love.
    Actually it's a flighty tween,
superficial and glittery. "Keep your eyes
    on the printed page; stop playing with your hair,"
I tell it, "and put down your portable screen!"
    No use. I'm supposed to profess
        that maturity is a gift,
but I don't believe it, or else don't care.
    I amble the library stacks and get lost in YA;
I want to go home, paint my nails until they iridesce,
    clamp on my headphones, and pray to Taylor Swift.

(Epigram 10)

Μικρή τις, Διόνυσε, καλὰ πρήσσοντι ποιητῇ

The poets who win a contest
almost
always say nothing about it. The others work hard,
having brooded at length on the sclerotic process,
to explicate the inequities of access,
the nepotism, the marked cards.
They are right today. They are right every day.
Poetry isn't a series of personal bests;
it's more like a kiln, or a room full of lobster tanks.
Nevertheless I write; I won't blame my tools.
When the lists, and the finalists
are announced, I'll know the rules,
and hope I can say just a few words of thanks.

(frag. 471)

Μοῦσαί νιν ἑοῖς ἐπὶ τυννὸν ἔθεντο

One of the Muses took this singer,
    in early childhood, onto her lap,
and he never got up, or even stood up,
    after that. His immediate failure
to cry or protest
    now seems, to us, a kind of harbinger,
or else a test,
    or else a lure.
Only in her arms would he feel secure.

(*Aetia*, book 1, frag. 2)

Ποιμένι μῆλα νέμοντι παρ᾽ ἴχνιον ὀξέος ἵππου

Sometimes you don't want it.
    When the Muse met Hesiod
under the star-sign of the horse,
    she told him, "Stop competing
with your rivals. Whatever you already have, don't flaunt it.
    Don't do anything that would improve your lot
by making others worse.
    And avoid the open-air market;
keep to your flock. Comb each of your ewes daily,
    no, four times a day. Develop a greeting
fit for companions soft as drowsing rugs,
    and subtler than whatever your lyre meant:
a kind of humblebrag, or a song of retirement,
    composed of nods and shrugs,
and sadder-but-wiser looks, and spitting, and bleating."

(Iambs, frag. 222)

οὐ γὰρ ἐργάτιν τρέφω

You shouldn't make children work all the time.
   Really you shouldn't do that to anyone,
but especially not to a kid.
   I wouldn't do that to my Muse,
though Simonides did.

(Iamb 3, frag. 193)

Εἴθ᾽ ἦν, ἄναξ ὤπολλον, ἡνίκ᾽ οὐκ ἦα

Apollo, lord of my only art, mouse god,
    plague tamer, you gave
me quite a task.
    Sometimes I wish I could live
long ago: you would have let me
    pray and bow to Cybele, sharing combs
with your other daughters, all of us hiding our lashes
    behind our glitter-spattered hair,
making up love songs and dirges about Adonis,
    who could have been one of us.
It doesn't seem like a big ask.

Instead I was born
    here and now, into
this body: an easy mark
    for the Muses who serve you. Sometimes I feel
like margarine for your clay-oven bread,
    compared to better girls' butter. Sometimes
accomplishing your work, my only work,
    feels less like opening an oven door,
or churning new milk, and more
    like polishing, or putting on, a mask.

(frag. 612)
ἀμάρτυρον οὐδὲν ἀείδω

Everything I set down has a source
    in prior song or the written record.
Some poets don't want to read first;
    some of us want to give the stories we know
a longer life, though none of us hopes
    to be regarded as just a quiz master or typist,
whose work is a game of hide-and-seek, or an echo.

(Epigram 29)

Ἡσιόδου τό τ᾽ ἄεισμα καὶ ὁ τρόπος· οὐ τὸν ἀοιδὸν

> Henry's new poems sound a lot like Hesiod's.
>> Not just his attitude, but his turn of phrase,
> his cadence, and, in fact, his actual words.
>> I wonder if Henry thinks the gods
> will reward
>> his choice. I wonder if he stays
> up late and asks if he could be that
>> artist who captured the feel of our works and days,
> or whether he'll get called out for what
>> he is: another clever copycat.

(Epigram 7)

Τοῦ Σαμίου πόνος εἰμὶ δόμῳ ποτὲ θεῖον ἀοιδὸν

Attribution is weird and scholars get it wrong.
　　For instance (this is inscribed
　　　　on a title page) my author is Crephylos,
who once met the actual Homer.
　　My story is the legend of King
　　　　Eurytus, who let
　　his daughter suffer such a famous loss,
Ione the copper-haired, the sunlight-clad.
　　My plethora of epithets long
　　　　meant my song
　　was credited
to the creator of the *Iliad*,
　　a flattering mistake, but a misnomer.

(Epigram 60)

Εὐδαίμων ὅτι τἄλλα μανεὶς ὠρχαῖος Ὀρέστας

Lucky Orestes.
        If you know his story,
you probably think that saying so makes me a jerk.
Fair enough. But I've been losing my mind
in my own way this week: Orestes lost his,
but at least he didn't insist
on asking his loyal companion to read and critique
his own book-length original fictional work.
That's why he kept Pylades as his friend.
True friendship can exist.
                As for me,
I need to learn how not to speak,
when not to hit send.

(from Hymn 2: To Apollo)

The bitter god called Envy tried to get under
    Apollo's skin.
"Only the strongest poets," Envy said,
    "deserve to be remembered; the prophets, the epic ones,
who turn their art form upside down.
    It's the same way with the ocean;
the sliding waves, the days of gentle rain
    erase one another, but the hurricanes,
the truly great floods—they alter the landscape
    permanently. Only they do work that counts."

Apollo considered ignoring Envy, then didn't,
    speaking up in order to set an example.
"Regular rain, and gentle rain," he said,
    "is what you want when caring for a crop,
and drinking water comes from handsbreadth springs.
    Miniatures deserve better.
Floods carry garbage, overrun storm drains, topple
    band shells and mansions, undermine human endeavor,
and make it hard to hear the Muses sing."

(Iambs, frag. 215)

ἥτις τραγῳδὸς μοῦσα ληκυθίζουσα

He was in one of those bands that use so much reverb
    you can't—at least if you're me—know
what the singer is saying.

I think he must think it makes him seem important,
    or tragic,
or emo.
He's more like a bilious pelagic

mammal with his blowhole blocked. If you want
    me to take you seriously,
or seek the right lever

to move me, keep it clear
    and spare,
with plenty of sunlight and air. Pretend
you're welcoming a guest. Sound like you're playing.

(Epigram 56)

Τῷ με Κανωπίτᾳ Καλλίστιον εἴκοσι μύξαις

When I began writing, I felt like a constellation,
    some new fixture in the sky,
a lamp with twenty wicks, or at least
    an eternal flame. It was mostly a lie
I told myself, though a few
    of my friends bought into it. Now
look at what I've become. I am, at best,
    a slender candle under glass,
a strip of magnesium you might
    ignite for a demonstration in chemistry class,
or else a meteorite, fast
    becoming invisible, something you could point out
to a child, a faint
    impression, a line that everyone knows can't last.

(Epigram 28)

Εἶχον ἀπὸ σμικρῶν ὀλίγον βίον οὔτε τι δεινὸν

Cover me quietly, stone.
I wrote verse. I meant little in life,
blamed few and injured none;
I tried to get along.
My writings kept me warm.
If I with my featherlight pen
confused prestige with worth,
praised evil, or ever wronged
the few who wanted a fight,
allow me, generous earth,
to do no further harm—
let me atone in my sleep;
I with my good will,
so lightly and often given,
who rest with nothing to keep,
and nothing to offer heaven.

(Epigram 30)

Ἐχθαίρω τὸ ποίημα τὸ κυκλικόν, οὐδὲ κελεύθῳ

Bunting I like, but not Olson, or Bernstein, or Pound;
    I'm tired of flashy long poems
that mean whatever anyone wants them to mean.
I'm also tired of crowds,
    hate the Met as I hate Times Square,
and won't see movies everyone else has seen.
As for you, Lusianias,
    I wanted to get to know you. Then I heard
how many others have known you, and how well.
Tomorrow, in fact, I suspect
    you'll show yet another young man
why he's just the one for you, and how you can tell.

(Iamb 4, frag. 194)

Εἴς—οὐ γάρ;—ἡμέων, παῖ Χαριτάδεω, καὶ σύ

Once on the hill of Tmolus
a laurel tree and an olive got into a fight,
　　or rather the laurel decided to pick on the olive,
making a kind of susurrus with her new leaves
　　to get the older tree's attention,
then launching in.
　　"What house lacks me" (she said)
"across its lintel,
　　what priest of Apollo refuses to carry me?
The Pythian oracle reclines
　　on beds of my feuilletons,
and sets me on fire in order to see what she sees.
　　With Phoebus on my side I took away
the plague in Ionia. My fumes fit magic spells.
　　Worshippers raise me up in their round dance;
athletes and singers crave me as their prize,
　　and I am carried to Delphi in holy procession.
I am so holy that I am not allowed
　　to approach sites of mourning and of sorrow;
nobody wants to leave me in a grave,
　　whereas your wood, lowly olive,
is something to burn at funerals."

　　The laurel's oily rival
responded right away: "My lovely friend,
　　my swan, my wondrous, peerless,
gorgeous one, you don't understand.
　　At all. No honor is greater
than to go with the dead,
　　the casualties of battle,
white-haired ladies and men,
　　and all the others for whom
I witness their passage out of this life; my twigs
　　snap with pride over any path
that pallbearers and mourners choose to walk.
　　There is no holier sound
than that percussive music.
　　Better this role alone
than to be some game's prize.
　　That said, I am also a prize,

the one given in the Olympic
    Games, a higher place
than anything Delphi holds.
    I am not, however, given
to the loquacious, the versifying boasters
    for their amplitudinous ornamentation.
I'd rather shut up and listen." But then two doves
    who nest in the olive's branches spoke up: one asked,
"Who made the laurel? Who created the olive?"
    "What about the grape, the oak, the fir?"
"Pallas Athena made the olive: that's
    how she became patron of Athens,
winning her contest against the god of salt water."
    "But divine Apollo made the laurel.
Comparing origins isn't going to help."
    "What can you do with the berries that grow on laurel?
You can't eat them, or drink them, or even make jewelry.
    Olives, on the other hand . . . there's oil,
and tapenade, and pickling, and so much—
    they can even be used as solid measures,
or baked into something like bread in emergencies.
    As for Apollo, it was the curve of the olive's
trunk that gave much-needed rest
    to his mother and the mother of Artemis,
generous, vexed, long-hidden Leto."
                                        "We have a winner."
    The laurel shook. The olive let the wind
keep moving around her knotty trunk, at her own pace.
    Then a rosebush spoke up, or rather
had barely begun to speak, with her scratchy throat
    that took so long to clear, when the laurel
cut in: "You have no right
    to start comparing yourself to either of us.
You're not on our level. You've never been
    the gift of any god,
and when you try to speak, it's like burps in brass,
    far away, mixed with grunts and scrapes and baas."
                    But the olive let
    the wind move on at her own pace,
and seemed to tilt a low branch toward the earth,
    and both the doves turned back to their small nest.

5

(*Aetia,* book 4, frag. 112: epilogue)
ὅτ᾽ ἐμὴ μοῦσα

My Muses, my Graces, I'm tired.
    My teachers, who told me you would reward
my service, told the truth.
    You paid my electric bill. You brought me fresh fruit.
You gave me patience while I tuned
    that much-strung, much-plucked lyre.
I brought you roses, and songs
    and stories from my country; I began
with the history of the gods, and with explanations
    of why things are the way they are,
and when you got bored, I pretended the clouds
    were sheep,
and made up antagonists shepherds could overcome.

    But now that's done.
I know that everything's political,
    but I need a break
from shepherds and flocks and pastures, from gods founding cities
    and heroes and orators and gullible crowds.

We love and admire you, Muse
    of history, whose sisters met Hesiod
under the sign of the horse: please take
    a vacation, and come back
to us in better health,
    or at least with good news.

We admire you, too, holy lord of lords, great Zeus,
who looks after our great leaders in peace and war,
    or at least protects the incumbent.
My friends and I need more
    time to ourselves: we might just walk around
in one of our tiny gardens and chat about words,
    and sex, and cuisine, and collectibles, and maybe learn
what the obscure, archaic
    phrase "to have fun" meant.

(Epigram 63a)

Κυνθιάδες θαρσεῖτε, τὰ γὰρ τοῦ Κρητὸς Ἐχέμμα

Cheer up, goats!
                    Manny's bow,
which he used to bring so many of you low—
to send you, in fact, all the way down to Hades,
or wherever it is goats go—
now rests behind glass in our local temple,
where no other hunters will find
in it a good excuse to kill, or boast.
After he cleared your kind
from our gardens and commons, the goddess
told him his cull was ample,
and he quit hunting, being of sound mind.

(Epigram 63b)

Κυνθιάδες θαρσεῖτε, τὰ γὰρ τοῦ Κρητὸς Ἐχέμμα

Cheer up, malefactors!
                              Liz, who brought
so many of you down,
will never file another brief.
She's already retired.
Without her, all sorts of bad actors
will go on giving working people grief,
until a new prosecutor comes to town
to put the fear of God into their hearts,
or let the air out of their tires.

(Epigram 4)

Μὴ χαίρειν εἴπῃς με, κακὸν κέαρ, ἀλλὰ πάρελθε

I already know how your friends with the school-spirit hoodies
are jerks who won't accept me, who mock or spy
on me and mine Monday through Friday. Frankly, it's rough.
    Don't ask me what my fucking mood is.

At the end of the school day don't bother saying goodbye—
I'll say goodbye to you. I know what's in
your sour heart. You think I'm a joke, or a sin.
    Just shut your friends up, please. That would be more than enough.

(*Aetia*, book 4, frag. 100)

οὔπω Σκέλμιον ἔργον ἐΰξοον, ἀλλ᾽ ἐπὶ τεθμόν

Everybody wants to be the talent.
　　Nobody wants to be the one
to manage the place, and implement compromises
　　needed for everyone else to continue to function.

That's true around here, and also on Mount Olympus.
　　Consider this wooden plank,
whose knots resemble eyes, its shakes tan hair
　　and eyelashes: tradition at Samos says
before expert carvers existed, this board was regarded
　　as a true and holy image of Hera,

set in an altar and worshipped along with the rest,
　　much like the crude, or primitivist,
Athena at Lindos. Why?
　　The queen of Olympus, the wife of Zeus,
is also the gods' organizer,
　　their schedule maker, quartermaster, and carer.

The other gods perfect themselves; they choose
　　their fearsome or awesome self-presentation
in detail—whether beautiful or sublime,
　　violet-lidded, or plaited, or shining hair loose—
when they face a congregation.
　　She can't, or won't. She doesn't have the time.

(Epigram 38)

Ὁ Λύκτιος Μενίτας

> This bow
> was once Katie-Kate's. Yes, the Olympic hero,
> who used it as if she were born
> to hit every target. She told me once, between
> bull's-eyes, "The curve, the horn,
> the notch and the wrist rest,
> are in the hands of whatever gods exist.
> The fate of an arrow, though—that's up to you,
> as long as it's not your last."

(Epigram 59)

Τίς, ξένος ὦ ναυηγέ; Λεόντιχος ἐνθάδε νεκρὸν

What or who are you, whose nameplate reads Opportunity?
    Leo the astronaut found you here, gouged by red sand,
and built a red rock cairn to cover you.
    Grant him forgiveness, or spiritual immunity,
you who had finished your mission, and then some; pity
    him, if you can.
Soon he will have to leave you, and rise high above you,
    and wait for another year before he can stand.

(frag. 557, 586)

εἴτε μιν Ἀργείων χρῆν με καλεῖν ἀάτην
εἰ θεὸν οἶσθα

> Those who have known a god must know
> that a god can do anything,
> > or prevent anything from being done.
> Helen did not dishonor the Achaeans,
> whatever my rivals sing. If you're looking
> > for somebody to blame: she's not the one.

(Epigram 6)

Κόγχος ἐγώ, Ζεφυρῖτι, παλαίτερος· ἀλλὰ σὺ νῦν με

I'm an old nautilus egg case. I make a good toy,
  or conversation
    piece, for Arsinoë, as I did
      for Marianne.
When there was wind,
  I rode that wind over the waves, as I still can,
    and when that earnest deity
      named Serenity
governed the sea, I did all my own locomotion,
  rowing with my many feet. That's why
    I'm sometimes called an Argonaut,
      and why the name fits.
I make a very good toy, and it's not
  just because I shimmer under moonlight,
    not just because I pretend to remove
      shame, scars, griefs, fears,
and long-embedded regrets;
  as Arsinoë knows, it's generosity
    that animates me. Each curve
      and pocket in me can display
a gem, a stone, a petal, a lock of hair,
  or some other token of friendship or love
    exchanged. I could
      be kept in a drawer,
but shouldn't be. Learning to play
  with me for more than a little
    while means learning to share.

(Epigram 5)

Τίμων, οὐ γὰρ ἔτ᾽ ἐσσί, τί τοι, σκότος ἢ φάος ἐχθρόν

Timon, you were part of an institution
    famous for passing judgment on everyone,
and finding almost all not good enough.
    Now that you're dead, is being dead a solution?
"Certainly not. So many people are dead;
    there are more under the earth than under the sun,
so many I can't reject them all. It's tough."

(Epigram 49)

Εὐμαθίην ᾐτεῖτο διδοὺς ἐμὲ Σῖμος ὁ Μίκκου

My first teacher prayed
    to the Muses that I should be a lover
of learning. They must have decided
    it was a good trade,
a force multiplier. Now I do the math
    in my grade
books; now I feign undivided
    attention (I probably look like a plaster
Dionysus, open-mouthed or
    yawning) as each so-talented
student recites their memorized part.
    I wish I could take cover:
instead I hear "The wrath
    of Achilles, sing, Muse" and "The art
of losing isn't hard
    to master," over
and over and over and over and over.

(Iamb 5, frag. 195)

Ὦ ξεῖνε—συμβουλὴ γὰρ ἕν τι τῶν ἱρῶν

You've been my friend for a while. You know you can trust me.
　　You know I consider education worthwhile.
And now that you're teaching middle school
　　for who knows how long, I'd like to help you see in it
something more than divine punishment.
　　You're going to smolder inside, sometimes. I know.
We all have. It's an archaic frustration. But if
　　the fire inside you isn't a firestorm, won't
burn forests to charcoal, and needs to be put down,
　　just tamp it down yourself. Try to hold your horses,
rather than chasing them more than once
　　around their own track. You'll just end up cracking your skull
on the first tight curve. Some lesson that would be,
　　and nothing new.
Don't laugh at me and I won't laugh at you.

(Epigram 34)

Οἶδ᾽ ὅτι μοι πλούτου κενεαὶ χέρες, ἀλλά, Μένιππε

For the sake of Laura Jane Grace and all the graces,
Mona, don't tell me how broke I am. I am
    quite aware of it.
That's almost as rude
    as telling someone her own dream,
as pointless as spelling out pi to twelve decimal places.
    If you're really worried, you could
always buy me some food,
    or find me appropriate work, so I could take care of it.

(*Hecale*, frag. 288 and 304)

Σκύλλα γυνὴ κατακᾶσα καὶ οὐ ψύθος οὔνομ᾽ ἔχουσα
ἀμφὶ δέ οἱ κεφαλῇ νέον Αἱμονίηθεν

    We all made fun of Celia when we learned that her name meant "hair."
    I used to think it wasn't fair.
    Then, at the end of history class, she took a pair of scissors
      to Niles' blazing purple undercut.
    I hope she gets caught without her coat in a blizzard.
      We took Niles straight to Harmony,
    their favorite shop, and bought them a hat.
      It's snug and round and warm and just as violently
    violet as the locks they lost,
        and Niles loves it. (Don't ask what it cost.)

(*Hecale*, frag. 282)

ὀκκόσον ὀφθαλμοὶ γὰρ ἀπευθέες, ὅσσον ἀκουή

Eyes take what's seen and rarely ask for more.
So trust your ears, and give to NPR.

(Iamb 8, frag. 198)

Ἀργώ κοτ᾽ ἐμπνέοντος ἤκαλον νότου

Gentle wind from the south that meant we were coming home
And also fresh water.

(*Aetia*, frag. 178)
ἠὼς οὐδὲ πιθοιγὶς ἐλάνθανεν οὐδ᾽ ὅτε δούλοις

Our people have our own holidays,
    which we observe when traveling.
It was on Grey's day that I first met Lynn,
    who used another name then; she had come
to Egypt for some sort of financial reason.
    I never asked for details. We hadn't met,
but as the saying goes, "We were strangers in Egypt."
    (If you don't know: I literally live in Egypt.)
She ended up staying at my place to avoid
    one of those horrific white-collar workplace parties
where all of the dudes get smashed. You know the type.
    A friend of a friend called and told me she needed
a place to crash, stat. So we had a few glasses of wine
    on my couch, and I think she was afraid
I'd come on to her, which I did not want to do.
    Seriously, you don't do that
to somebody who has no place to go.
    (Really, dudes.) Instead, I asked her about
her own sacred days. Why do your people
    worship the Cyclops, for example, and mourn
his epic death one day each year?
    And then she told me the story. You would not believe
how long it took. When she was all done
    it was practically dawn. I remember saying "You're lucky:
you can find some of your people wherever you go."
    And she said, "I guess. But I think you're lucky
if you never board an airplane; as for me,
    I see myself in kittiwakes and terns—
if I feel at home
    anywhere, it's over water,
practically soothed by jet engines,
    trying to get some sleep
by counting the curves in the waves."

6

(Epigram 46)

"Ληφθήσει, περίφευγε, Μενέκρατες" εἶπα Πανήμου

I lost my friend's laptop. I thought about skipping town
　　so she wouldn't skin me alive.
That was June 20. On the tenth of July
　　it just
turned up in a pile of clipboards and three-ring binders.
　　Oh Hermes, my
good god, my prankster and finder
　　of lost
possessions, I won't ask why
　　you took so long. I'm just glad it's here now.

(Iamb 9, frag. 199)

Ἑρμᾶ, τί τοι τὸ νεῦρον, ὦ Γενειόλα,

Hermes, you've definitely been around for a while,
guarding our stoops, gates, foyers, and front yards;
at least this version of you has. Look at that beard
on you. But look at your sensitive part.
It's pointed up, towards your moustache, let's say,
rather than at your feet in the common style.
No wonder: stuck in that stance, all day, every day,
you can't ever touch it. You must have had some thoughts
about the people you've seen. Of course it's hard.

(Epigram 26)

Ἥρως Ἠετίωνος ἐπίσταθμος Ἀμφιπολίτεω

I am a superhero with mask, gloves, and boots on,
    an action figure who comes with a burger and fries.
      You can bend
my elbows and knees, or pretend
    force beams come out of my ruby-tinted eyes.

Once, the station
    or corner of rug I defend
      would have been a GI's,
or a straight-shooting sheriff's; but I was made for a nation
    where guns are neither a toy, nor a surprise.

(Epigram 57)

Φησὶν ὅ με στήσας Εὐαίνετος (οὐ γὰρ ἔγωγε

I'm an enamel pin with a black-and-yellow
    superhero logo.
I have no clue who might be wearing me,
but Shelby, who made me, promised me I would go
    only to somebody worthy
of the image of my hero
(a sturdy ally, perhaps, or a friend of Dorothy),
    not just to any schmo or bro or no-show.

(Epigram 48)

Τὴν ἁλίην Εὔδημος, ἐφ' ἧς ἅλα λιτὸν ἐπέσθων

By using no spice but salt,
Eudemus, once in debt—
hence mortal peril—changed
his ways, and saved his skin
from creditors' long knives.
Now kept afloat by thrift
as sailors by a raft,
he therefore consecrates
this saltcellar to what
gods—humble and without
high monuments—permit
his business to go on.

(Iamb 7, frag. 197)

Ἑρμᾶς ὁ Περφεραῖος, Αἰνίων θεός,

I am the deity of the periphery,
      patron of invention and escape,
whose sacred animal is the chameleon,
      or else the artificial stallion
that led to the fall of Troy,
      devised by my first
lay priest, a tinker from Phocis
      famous for being no good in a scrape.

(*Aetia*, frag. 115)

λάθρη δὲ παρ᾽ Ἡφαίστοιο καμίνοις

on the gods of Samothrace

There are more than two, and they work in secret,
    where winters are cages of ice and summer
        a gauntlet of heat.
They do not live on Olympus, but have learned from Hephaestus
    how to make a shield that can last forever
        out of a man-sized sheet
of iron, and opalescent helical bracelets
    out of a rainbow and a meteorite.
They are the allies of refugees, and of shape-shifters,
    and can easily pummel those
who threaten their companions, whether with fists or
    red-hot hammers; but they would much rather
        fashion more of their favorite things than fight.

(Epigram 52)

Τέσσαρες αἱ Χάριτες· ποτὶ γὰρ μία ταῖς τρισὶ τήναις

There were four Graces. There are not.
　　The fifth protects the players and playing of games,
and is newly anointed; she stands out
　　　　for the lives she has saved. Her names
are Berenice, Phoebe, and Lea. She's never alone.
　　The others rely on her. She cherishes her own,
fears cut scenes, and grants infamy, or fame,
　　　　since grace
requires choice; it is she
　　　　to whom you pray
if you harbor fears, or have been tempted to say,
　　　　that no matter what you do, the world is the same.

(*Hecale*, frag. 261)

ἡ μὲν ἀερτάζουσα μέγα τρύφος ὑψίζωνος

Of course Athena does not date men.
　　　Rivals say she's jealous, but she's not:
she has no trouble working with them,
　　　keeping their secrets, even,
　　　　　if that's best.
She makes the plans the others want to follow.

This morning, as dawn turned everything violet,
　　　then red-orange, then ripe-apple yellow,
I saw her in her peacetime daytime dress,
　　　whose linen drops over one shoulder, climbing the steps
to the sunlit outdoor center-city workspace,
　　　the one with the gold columns,
　　　　　early to meet Apollo.

(*Hecale*, frag. 299, 301)
Αἴσηπον ἔχεις, ἑλικώτατον ὕδωρ,
βουσόον ὅν τε μύωπα βοῶν καλέουσιν ἀμορβοί

The goddess we call our foe
    but sing for, all the same,
the only goddess who knows
    what, if any, grain will grow
this year if we sow
    that particular grain's saved seeds, and whether the sea
will remain in its own shallow
    furrows or swallow
our seaside town: we call her by one name
    and then another, Nemesis
and Justice, Fortune and Chance,
    and Merit and Randomness,
as well as May and Could and Should
    and Possibility and Might.

She is (may she look kindly
    on the comparison) like the bright
horsefly, whose bite
    cows loathe,
that hovers and bothers your already
    sweaty face,
that cowherds know as ornery
    but on occasion necessary
for employment and even
    for survival; without its
annoyance as
    spur, the cattle would stay
where they are, and never
    let humans drive them
from place to place.

(*Aetia*, book 2, frag. 43)

καὶ γὰρ ἐγὼ τὰ μὲν ὅσσα καρήατι τῆμος ἔδωκα

The soft hats I brought back from my travels
    got chewed up—they look almost threadbare—
thanks (but no thanks) to the boat ride home,
    which also broke the goblets in my luggage.
As for what I enjoyed with palate and tongue—
    it's not like anyone could bring that back.
I can, however, say what I saw and heard.

I saw Leontini, where visitors trace
two fingers across the sea-foam;
    I saw the island Megara, named by Megarians
who ought to have called it New Megara, since
    they came from the mainland to built
a miniature form of their old life.
    Its temples hold genealogies carved into pediments;
no planner of bridge or wall goes anonymous there.
    I took a long stroll in the sun-blessed city
of Gelas, whose smooth schist gates name its founders,
    sons of Crete and sons of Rhodes.

And then there is Zanton. Help me, Clio,
Melpomene, Thalia too, as I try
    to clarify: the thing
that baffles travelers in Zanton
    is that no resident will ever tell
(tradition prohibits it, though it's not strictly illegal)
    the whole story of how it came to be.
And yet you can piece it, or most of it, together,
    by listening to the citizens, if you're careful
and checking out both sides when they disagree.

The settlers came from Kume and Khalkis,
led by the captains Perieres
    and Krataimenes, who called himself the Victor
(he had good reason, given where he'd fought).
    No sooner did they land in Sicily
than they began to erect, and to fortify, walls;
    they never laid the herb mesh, nor did they spread the celery leaves

that would have kept off the harpies,
    or else attracted a heron to chase them away.
You on the mainland have probably never seen
    harpies, and lucky you if so:
their shadows shelter slanderers; the trails
    their filthy feathers turn children sad
or disobedient, and seeds to sterile dust
    before they're sown. Those same birds' iron talons
buckle pavements, and—adding injury
    to injury—their presence makes routine maintenance
next to impossible: nauseated citizens
    refuse to pay their tax—
mistrustful and badly nourished, they can't see past today.
    If you ever have the misfortune to launch a colony,
do not settle where the harpies land.

For Zanton, though, it was too late. Muses, let me say
    what I could uncover there.
After the walls went up, the captains claimed
    that all the roads and walks, planks, stairs, and gates
and even the balances that kept merchants fair,
    defended them from some external foe,
the made-up marines of some navy a few tides away.
    All lies, of course, but the only way—
that duo believed—to hold the place together.
    Then Perieres and Krataimenes set,
below the main fortification, a granite pot
    whose silver plastron held the scythe of Kronos,
the titan who castrated his father the sky.

    You have to understand that it was dangerous—
blasphemous, even—to approach the scythe,
    or even admit its existence.
Supposedly Zeus would slam his bolts right at it
    the moment blade saw sky.
Where did Perieres, or Krataimenes,
    unearth it? how could it travel with them? Who knows?
But it worked; the harpies, who can see
    through leather, steel, or stone, shook and took fright
at the hard and ancient sovereign reminder
    of violence that made their violence

petty and inconsequential. In one last
   eruption of alkaline fumes, they flapped away.

Proud of the stratagem, wanting the credit
   for saving the town, each man
hoped to rename it for himself.
   Perieres wanted to keep the shrine
forever secret. Krataimenes preferred
   to reveal it and launch a feast
to honor what grim magic kept them safe.
   Today, they might have formed political parties.
Instead, they nearly drew knives
   and tried to stab each other. Then they agreed
to ask divine Apollo instead. They climbed
   the pebbly hills, each lugging bags of leaves,
crushed laurel they were meant to strew and burn.
   But the chapel, the acolytes
and the redolent outdoor altar
   presented only silence, which they took
as itself an answer—never tell
   the whole tale; never, moreover, name
the founders of the town: "a sacred veil
   is to be drawn over the beginnings
of all governments." Or at least this one here.

And so even now, even on sacred days,
the city, its peacock markets, and its docks
   so close to the bourse, its reciters and lutenists,
seed vendors, rhetoric teachers, and resident priests
   refuse to say the name of either man.
In fact, they prefer to avoid even naming the town,
   whose name on maps means something like "sickle" or "scythe."
When the deputy mayors announce
   the annual civic feast, they say,
"May the majestic initiators
   of our metropolitan way of life—
whoever they were; we really have no idea,
   it was so long ago—grace our revels and green our fields;
we honor whatever they did or might have done."
   They roast at least two oxen, and their round cakes,
though slightly burnt, taste sweet, with basil and lime.

(*Aetia*, frag. 177)
ἀστὴρ δ᾽ εὖτ᾽] ἄρ᾽ ἔμελλε βοῶν ἄπο μέσσαβα

Some inventions are simple
delights. But there are others
    whose operations we'd rather not see.
Did you know, for example,
    that holy Apollo devised
the first mousetrap? I'll tell you how and why.
    The god once disguised himself
as a poor man. He slept in a hut,
    with a goat's-hair blanket for his cloak,
and a sack for storing flatbread.
    When the god awoke, very early,
on a rainy day, he heard
    what he thought were raindrops. Then he felt
the mouse toes on his forehead. It was gross.
    Of course
he couldn't get back to sleep. And even worse,
    the tiny thieves had eaten through that cloak,
and ate all the seeds in his seed sack, and gnawed holes
    in his undershirt, like a plague of moths.

Apollo is, when he wishes, a god
    of wrath.
That evening, when he was walking home
    from his uncommonly lengthy wanderings,
at the same time as the sunset told the oxen
    they, too, would soon go home,
and told the crepuscular nymphs
    they could come out and play,
protected by the dome
    that shields them from the sun,
when Apollo himself felt ready to shut
    his eyes, and place a rock by his front door,
there was that scrabble again. Paws. House mice.
    It was like when young deer catch the spoor
of a predator,
    except in reverse. The god struck
and missed. "Go away
    forever," he told them. "You're the worst.

I'll be the last
      you molest,
you with your tiny ears and twitchy nose
      and clammy paws and uncannily flexible
tail that goes
      wherever you go, pest. If I let
you multiply unchecked,
      you may eat the whole world's grain,
from barley and wheat to quadrotriticale,
      Then human hospitality will fail;
you and your snouts will have come
      between each host and every guest."

Then Apollo paused in reciting his curse
      and picked up sticks, to entice
the mice out of hiding, and end them.
      He mixed up flour with honey and powdered lime.
He became their herald of death,
      leaving corpses in house corners.
He saw them dip the tips of their tails
      in lamp oil, and lick them
for the fat on them, and so he scattered phosphide
      dust below the brass lip of the lamp.
Mice are annoying enough
      to a god, thought the god; imagine what they must
do to a needy householder, with no refuge
      up in the clouds, and no way to hide.

Mouse Lord, or Mouse Slayer
      he is sometimes called.
He set out to kill, and taught human beings how to kill
      mice in two more ways,
one with a hinge that snaps shut
      the other like a trebuchet,
its lever sprung from behind.
      Let nobody say he cannot work his will.
And yet there are mice on Earth,
      today and every day, still,
as if the god had changed his mind.

(Hymn 6: To Demeter)

Lift up the basket for the harvest festival.
    Lift it up so we see how heavy it is,
so that we see it from below.
    See the bristles of wheat,
the sacks and husks of barley.
    See how much our farmers grow.

We see the basket on this day, a feast,
    as we saw it yesterday, a fast
when we all had to wait for Eve,
    that is, the divinity Evening,
who persuaded Demeter to drink
    sweet water after she had refused to drink,
or eat, without her missing child.

That's not a story we need to hear again.
    Demeter has been a mother
who wept over her daughter;
    she's also a badass, a goddess
who keeps our cities whole.
    She's been a lawgiver; she gave
our assemblies rules for civil
    and fair debate; she gave
our cultivators rules
    for sorting sheaves of wheat
and plowing, and knowing what field
    to leave fallow and when; and she gave human beings
the lore that lets us care for our laboring animals,
    burly oxen, eager hens, calm sheep.

Also she punishes greed.
    Let's hear that story. Near
Knidos, in Marcadotia,
    the Pelasgians (who elect their kings) set up
what we now call a nature preserve,
    a small one, really a grove,
close-packed with flowering trees,
    so close you could not shoot an arrow through:
mammoth elms, sweet apples
    and quinces on flourishing bushes,

plums and date-plums, with their amber bark
    like waterfalls, and beech, and hard brown pears.
Demeter loved it more than she could say.

Erysichthon was both a merchant
    and a literal prince,
a trader in grains and wood. One day his rivals
    in Marcadotia cut him out of a deal
in hardwood futures. He grew enraged.
    He hired a team of twenty laborers
and expert woodsmen, buying each an ax,
    to cut down the whole of the grove.
He hungered for his own supply.

At the edge of that grove, there grew
    one poplar, mature and hefty, with leaves
held up, as supplicants do, to the sky.
    The tree had his own wood nymphs,
companions to Demeter and her friends,
    who lounged in his branches at snack time
and raced up the trunk at noon.
    Erysichthon's men
attempted to cut him down first.
    The poplar screamed—a grating,
unmistakable scream.
    The axe stuck in his trunk.

    Demeter noticed, of course.
She gave herself the face of Nicola,
    her Marcadotian priest
who led her weekly sacrifice in town,
    and spoke, to Erysichthon, soothing words:
"My child, my prince, stop and listen
    to the wind that's sifting through these trees.
They are my holy trees. I set them apart.
    My child, stop. Give yourself time,
and space, and take a rest.
    Consider your parents' prayers,
and tell your workers to stop.
    You need not cut down everything you see.
Don't treat this grove,
    or anything planted that grows, like some enemy town

you have to sack. That's not how nature works.
    I'm warning you politely. Don't provoke me—
that is, I mean, do not anger my patron,
    the goddess Demeter. You wouldn't like her when she's—"

But Erysichthon wouldn't listen.
    He looked back at her the way a crouching lion
looks at a hunter in the Dodonian hills,
    a lion who just gave birth, with cubs to protect.
"Don't take my ax away from me," he said,
    "or it might land in you.
It's mine. These groves are mine.
    The market has spoken. I'm sorry you're not satisfied.
And by the way, girl,
    before you run back to your shrine in the center of town,
know that I wasn't planning to strip and sell
    these fruit trees' wood; I need it for myself,
to build" (he meant something like "pay or cause others to build")
    "the kind of house someone like me deserves,
where my wife and I and our family can entertain.
    Or don't you value family? No, you wouldn't,
you and your posse of girls
    who don't even own your homes."

Then Demeter shed her shape
    so that she appeared as a god,
the soles of her feet on the soil,
    her forehead as high and far away
(or so it seemed, then) as Olympus.
    The hired woodsmen took one look
and ran away, axes in trees;
    Demeter let them go. Erysichthon,
on the other hand . . . she had words for him.
    "Build your fancy mansion, hungry dog,
and hold your dinner parties while you can.
    That house will see a lot of feasts,
and soon." Then
    she was gone.

By the time he got home Erysichthon was hungry.
    Very hungry. Burningly, blindingly hungry.

The kind of hunger you get when you've just been ill
  and exhausted and languid and suddenly you feel better,
except that he didn't feel better. Nothing was enough.
  He hired twenty cooks, and twenty butlers,
and sent away for casks and casks of wine.

  Another lovely fact about Erysichthon:
despite his boasts about home ownership,
  about how the market had made him the sole
master of himself,
  he lived with his mother and father, who now tried
to keep him away from parties and social occasions,
  for fear he'd eat the guests. Can Erysichthon
attend the Athenian games?
  "I'm sorry," his mother said. "He's not at home;
he's cutting a deal in ox tongues. Come again
  next week?" The lady Polyxa
invited Erysichthon and his dad
  to an island wedding. "My husband Trey will come.
Erysichthon, though—he'd love to go,
  but he got rushed by a boar
on one of his hunting trips; you know how much
  he loves to hunt, he's so brave,
but he's on bed rest for the next nine days."
  She loved her son. She kept trying
to appease him, and shovel food at him. She kept him at home,
  and kept on lying about it.

"Sorry, he's got a concussion."
  "Sorry; as you know,
he's a major investor in poultry,
  and had to examine the stock."
Of course he stayed at home all day,
  just eating.
It was like tipping those trucks of snow
  into the mother of rivers
after the great snowstorms of the Middle West;
  no matter how much there is
to begin with, it all goes away,
  and fast. That's what it was like for Erysichthon,
shoving steaks, rolls, grapes, grape leaves, and wedges of cabbage,
  boiled or roasted or raw, between his teeth.

His body, meanwhile, grew thin,
    like traces of snow on a mountain
whose peak is exposed to the sun.
    You could see his ribs;
you could see his shoulder blades.
    His mother wept. His sisters wept.
His father Trey wept too,
    but not for the same reason. Trey complained,
"My life would be easier if I could bury him now,
    if he just died of sunstroke, or drowned in the waves.
Instead he's eating everything I own."

Trey's son ate the mules. He ate the whole of the cow
    his mother was saving to sacrifice for Hestia,
down to the knucklebones and the large intestines.
    He ate the racehorse, and the warhorse, and the cat.
(Mice ran through that house, less afraid. And then he ate them.)
    When there was no meat,
no bread, no beer, no wine, no stalks, no beans,
    he chewed on ladles, on brooms,
on shoes, on bricks, on empty pots, on swords,
    or swallowed household powders. He knocked
most of his teeth out, trying to eat
    one durable household object at a time.
If it sounds hilarious,
    try living with someone like that. The curse was real,
the family bankruptcy also real.
    When last seen the son of Trey was spending his days
far from his former home, where three roads meet,
    panhandling, dumpster diving. The market had spoken.
The goddess had spoken, too, with her just voice.

Lift up the basket for the harvest festival.
    Lift it up so that we see how heavy it is,
so that we see it from below.
    Demeter, may my own friends treat you well,
and never lay claim to what is not their own.

As the four horses of our ceremony
    take up the holy basket,
so may the four seasons keep us safe,
    and safely fed,

and may they bring us gold, not enough
    for everything we want,
but rather enough to keep us all from want.
    Let the parade lead us all
to City Hall,
    where taxes also go, to feed the poor,
and those of us who can easily climb
    the sixty steps will ascend
to Demeter's inner shrine
    (the shrine's old stairs are older than our laws);
those who cannot: she will bless you
    where you are.

Demeter, keep us from greed,
    and keep our men from feeding on themselves;
give us agronomy, and ripe bell peppers,
    and justice, and soft, calm sheep, and ears of wheat
enough for all our bread,
    and let the bakers walk to work in safety,
especially those who come from far away,
    as our procession comes from far away
and ends in our own town square.
    Whether we call on you, goddess,
for sustenance or safety
    or justice, let us always
find you there.

7

(*Aetia,* book 4, frag. 103)

Ἥρως ὦ κατὰ πρύμναν, ἐπεὶ τόδε κύρβις ἀείδει

> The pillar at the dock must sing his song
>   about heroes, his long
> farewell, to the stern;
>   the last part
> of each ship to depart,
>   and the last to return.

(frag. 714)

κουφοτέρως τότε φῶτα διαθλίβουσιν ἀνῖαι

Why do I write? Experience
    and scientific evidence agree:
an otherwise intolerable load
    of shame decreases by up to six percent
if told to even a temporary companion,
    through a folded-up page at recess, a performance
on classical guitar, a palinode,
    a Tumblr, or a hash mark on a tree;
fears diminish, at least a little, whenever secrets
    are no longer secrets and enter the common
atmosphere, even as birdsong, even in code.

(*Hecale*, frag. 278)

τοὔνεκα καὶ νέκυες πορθμήιον οὔτι φέρονται

Don't let yourself or your friends or your children leave
    the house without money.
That rule extends to the dead,
    who have to cross the Styx.
The citizens of this one town, however,
    (who asked me to keep its name secret) will lower
their neighbors into the grave
    without a cent in their pockets, in their mouths,
or over their dried-up eyes.
    Their ancestors told Demeter
where she could find her daughter,
    and the goddess of all harvests gave
their descendants free passage over that river: their
    perpetual and melancholy prize.

(Iamb 13, frag. 203)

Μοῦσαι καλαὶ κἄπολλον, οἷς ἐγὼ σπένδω

I'm not exactly from poverty, or from obscurity,
but I think it's OK for me to complain.

Some people treat the right, or the ability
to make, or to talk about, poetry

as a matter of being born in the right place,
or as some kind of laying on of hands.

Just because your town is known for tragedies,
they tell you that's what you must write,

as if creating superheroes, or love songs,
were like not minding the store.

But you're not a peon
for liking what you like. Stop keeping score.

You don't need the gods' permission
to mix things that have never mixed before.

As for the ones who want purity,
they think they're being delicate,

but really they're passing up delicacies
on unfamiliar trees,

and climbing up withered and tall ones to pluck famine food.
No wonder they're in a bad mood.

They remind me of the mainlanders
who would not let Leto give birth.

(Still to this day we get so much from islands,
where villages have little choice:

either they keep up feuds forever, or else
they mix and learn one another's worth.)

Some of us do need reminders to stay in our lane.
At the same time, if some set of words speaks to your heart,

makes you catch your breath, and scrambles your taste,
even if it confuses you—that's worthwhile.

Experiment. (But stay willing
to admit when experiments fail.)

Plant what you want to grow. (But bring your flail,
and pray to the Muses for rain.)

And critics: think twice before grabbing a bull's new horns,
before you get gored, or cause somebody else pain.

I'm not exactly from poverty, or from obscurity,
but I think it's OK for me to complain.

(*Hecale*, frag. 231)
τίον δέ ἑ πάντες ὁδῖται

From welcoming the stranger
    all other virtues flow.
Travelers will thank you
    if you keep a house that feels
as if it had no roof, and no locked door,
    and the gods will protect you,
though how and when? That's hard to know.

(Epigram 4)

Μὴ χαίρειν εἴπῃς με, κακὸν κέαρ, ἀλλὰ πάρελθε·

    Don't hold yourself superior to others.
Don't make fun of people for things they can't change,
    or else stop hanging out with me. Don't bother—
at the least, your inability
    to cool it with the mockery
bespeaks a certain failure of writerly range.

(*Aetia*, book 4, frag. 96)

Θεοὶ πάντες κομποῖς νεμεσήμονες, ἐκ δέ τε πάντων

The gods (to put it calmly) aren't big fans
    of people who boast about their education,
who swing one branch or medal around
    and treat it as their matchless qualification
for every future throne and crown.

    None of the gods are fans. But for Artemis—
whose mother was a refugee,
    who grew up alone in the woods—it's personal.
Tell her your school's pedigree
    means you go first in the hunt,
or (worse) that you must go in front
    of her and her maidens, and she'll place a call
to Nemesis,
    and they will find a way to bring you down.

(*Hecale*, frag. 358)

εἰ δὲ Δίκη σε

> Justice will give you your due,
> if not at once, then underground,
> where everybody on Earth, includ-
> ing everybody you wronged,
> will someday be found.

(frag. 467, 480, 491)
ἐδείμαμεν ἄστεα μορτοί
ἀρχόμενοι μανίην ὀξυτάτην ἔχομεν
μεῖον ἐδάκρυσεν Τρωίλος ἢ Πρίαμος

    We build cities and towns, we mortals. The deathless gods
       do not. Why?
                Desire, hope, focus, mania
    to accomplish something—call it what you will—
       are sharpest at the start, and among the young.
    Who lost more? Troilus, slain
       before he turned nineteen?
    Or the last king of Troy,
       who lived to see the end
    of his kingdom, his temple, and his youngest boy?

(Epigram 25)

Εἶπας "Ἥλιε χαῖρε" Κλεόμβροτος Ὠμβρακιώτης

"Goodbye to the sunlit world," said Klia, who took
    the leap before which nobody ever looks.
        Should we, her wrecked
      friends, stay angry at the adults
    who failed to protect her? Or at the dolt-
      ish clichés and the toxic myth
      that still obscure the durable intellects
of Plath, and Virginia Woolf, and Elliott Smith?

(Epigram 9)

Ἦλθε Θεαίτητος καθαρὴν ὁδόν. εἰ δ᾽ ἐπὶ κισσὸν

The singer who wrote the songs for the band Game Theory
    belongs in the heavens along
        with their greatest songs.
He wasn't a party guy. He never got famous
    enough to win a major prize.
During his life, he heard DJs name
    so many other artists, over and over.
But when your kids are trying to find their course
    amid false friends, or trying to recover
from the worst breakup ever in their short lives—
    it's his songs that are going to leave them teary,
his songs that will ring in their ears, and open their eyes.

(Epigram 11)

Τῇδε Σάων ὁ Δίκωνος Ἀκάνθιος ἱερὸν ὕπνον

Whatever happens happens for all time.
  Under this stone sleeps Saon,
the Acanthian, whose father was Dikon.
  who will not awaken again.
Don't say he's unremembered. (But now he'll never be mine.)

(*Hecale*, frag. 263)

ἴθι, πρηεῖα γυναικῶν

at Hecale's tomb

Nothing new will vex you or make you heartsick,
    first among women, on your final road.
We will remember you for your hospitality:
    strangers from far away who fled
bigotry, meanness, landslide, fire, and flood
    could come to you for warmth and food.

(Epigram 22)

Ἠῷοι Μελάνιππον ἐθάπτομεν, ἠελίου δὲ

Visual depictions of suicide kill.
We buried Melanie that morning;
the day after, Basil died.
I don't know what he saw,
or what she did, but I know
I've seen too many pictures of oblivion
done up as heaven.

This isn't a poem so much as a warning.
We're going to be sad for a while.
Yesterday I could hardly keep my head
up; I could barely see the road
through the tears. I had driven
past his building,
where his torn-up friends, and the friends of her friends,
are still living.

(Epigram 16)

Δαίμονα τίς δ' εὖ οἶδε τὸν αὔριον; ἀνίκα καὶ σέ

Nobody knows what the gods will bring tomorrow.
    Yesterday, Carol, we got to hang out with you.
The day after that we bury you. There's your father
    in his raincoat, chilled to the marrow,
motionless with sorrow.

(Epigram 17)

"Τιμονόη." τίς δ᾿ ἐσσί; μὰ δαίμονας, οὔ σ᾿ ἂν ἐπέγνων

When I am in cemeteries I consider
    people I never knew when they were alive.
Timothea, your smooth grave
    says only that you were named after your father,
and where you died, and when, and that Eugene,
    your husband, loved you after you were gone.

(Epigram 18)

Κρηθίδα τὴν πολύμυθον, ἐπισταμένην καλὰ παίζειν

Cress was the best kind of chatterbox. Her classmates
 would stay up till any hour
just to hear her sweet voice telling stories.
 I remember they would congregate
on her shag carpet and on the bedspread in her room.
 But every child needs to get enough sleep,
and now, I guess, she can catch up.
 Thanks to the wise divinities, in their wisdom.
No human being who heard her
 ever wanted her to stop.

(Epigram 21)
Δωδεκέτη τὸν παῖδα πατὴρ ἀπέθηκε Φίλιππος

Here lies Nicholas, the son
   of Philip, who buried him.
There is no hope in the world:
   so it seemed, that day, to his father. That's it. I'm done.

(Epigram 23)

Ὅστις ἐμὸν παρὰ σῆμα φέρεις πόδα, Καλλιμάχου με

the poet's father speaks

I named my son after his grandfather,
    Callimachus of Cyrene.
The first of that title to win Panhellenic fame
    defended his city in armor;
the second made deathless songs and epitaphs, some
    in character, or in somebody else's name.

So decreed Nemesis; so I should have predicted
from seeing him as a child, so often bent
    over some improvised writing implement,
a charcoal plug, or a wet reed, still green.
    In life I overlooked it. In death I miss it.
Now I know that "when the Muses visit
    a girl, or a schoolboy, they intend to stay,
or else to come back, even after the poet goes gray."

(*Hecale*, frag. 298)

ἐπεὶ θεὸς οὐδὲ γελάσσαι

The god who made us made us such
    that whenever you or anybody laugh,
someone is probably crying; someone got hurt.
    If the foreground is joy, the background is always sad.
I admit it's not much
    but it's something to say, on that poor god's behalf:
look what he had
    to work with. Look what we came from: water and dirt.

(*Hecale*, frag. 291)
ἡνίκα μὲν γὰρ †φαίνεται τοῖς ἀνθρώποις ταῦτα†

The same, single, visible, daily phenomenon
    enters our field of vision, the same
when the light starts to fail
    and we hail
it and it winks back slowly, low on the horizon,

the same when it returns at dawn to call
    a halt
to overlong sleep or a risky liaison.
    We hoped for it. Now we resent it. But it's the same.

(*Aetia*, book 1, frag. 23)

ἀστέρα, ναὶ κεραῶν ῥῆξιν ἄριστε βοῶν

Sometimes people won't listen. Sometimes they can't.
 As a peak
in the Carpathians pays no attention
 to a ripple in the Aegean,
as an A-list celebrity will not speak
 with any random Twitter admirer,
as an aggrieved third-grader
 pretends to ignore their father,
as devotees of Mahler
 find no time
for rockabilly, or twelve-tone, or grime—
 sometimes they can't; that's why they won't

It's easier for Heracles to follow
 Hera's punitive instructions,
easier to tell Hera what to do,
 than to compete with distractions
caused by love-longing, or children
 cuddling, or children yelling. You can't get through
to someone so wrapped up in their own thing,
 no matter how much your thing
means to you.

(Iamb 2, frag. 192)

Ἦν κεῖνος οὐνιαυτός, ᾧ τό τε πτηνόν

At one time all the animals—
    even the ones with hooves or feathers or gills—
could use words, as we do.
    That was when Kronos ruled. And though Zeus
is just, and his laws are just,
    he reserved language for us. In his reallocation,

he gave the vocal talents
    of foxes to politicians,
whales' phrases to tragedians,
    heralds the terms that used
to come from a hawk's beak,
    and so on. Which explains

why humans have so many voices within us.
    Other creatures don't know what they're missing.
No wonder it's so hard for us to close
    our lips and pay attention
to one another. No wonder we speak
    when we ought to listen.

(Hymn 5: To Athena)

It is not for me—gods forbid it—to watch
    Pallas bathe, this day of her ceremonial bath,
but I can praise her attendants anyway:
    I hear your horses snort their holy fire as they
slow to a trot, then stop
    and whinny as the goddess
ties them up, gently, herself.
    She cares about them. Even on the night she returned,
her normally shining arms all crust and sludge
    and blood, from hacking apart the malignant giants,
she stopped at the verge of her property to scrub the horses' necks,
    transferring the clean cold spray
from the sea god's ocean
    to clear sweat and foam from their ragged mouths.

Now she's coming back here. Don't bother to bring
    rose water, saffron, or verbena
(the rush of her wheels on their way shakes the dry ground).
    She won't need a mirror. She knows how fair she appears.
Even when she took part
    in that fancy-dress fiasco, the judgment on Ida,
she did not bring reflective bronze or glass.
    When she last went distance running, competing beside
those Spartan twins we now regard as stars,
    you polished her skin with olive leaves and oil.
Male champions like Castor—like Heracles, even—
    wear olive oil too. So bring
her olive oil again.
    Bring her aureate comb, so she can comb out her own hair.

    Athena! Your girls, your favorite pupils, are waiting,
the studious granddaughters of your half-brother Apollo.
    One of them brought you Diomedes' shield,
as custom and the priest Eumedes taught,
    Eumedes who, when he learned
about the plot against him, took two sacks,
    a cloak for himself in one, your idol in the other,
and ran off to set up his tent on your holy hill.

Let us hear you, Athena. You can be heard
    above the clash of hoplites and the mayhem
that makes smithereens out of bronze, and splinters from shields:
    tactician, concluder of wars, we are ready
to honor you in peace. We drew our own baths
    elsewhere last night, having saved for you
today's pellucid water from the spring.
    Protector of cities, come visit us; even the girls
whom you allow to help you will look away,
    making a cordon around you,
and while they await you I'll tell them a story I know.

*

Once, long ago, the goddess had one best friend,
    a human woman. They did everything together.
When Athena would drive
    around the city walls, past the split-levels
and the woods where now we have a school,
    past the amaranth field and the park the Boiotians made,
or up to her riverside altar
    at Coronéa with its thorny groves,
wherever she went, she brought that lady,
    named Coracle. Every sporting event,
every temple inspection, every poetry reading,
    they were together. Sometimes they held hands.
One day at noon the two of them folded their gowns
    and laid them beside the Heliconian spring,
the one we still call Colt's Spring, since it runs so fast,
    and each one seemed to help the other lower
her body into the sunlit water.
    There was no shade, and no cover, but no one around,
and, for who knows how long, no sound.
    Then a teenaged boy and a terrier,
running towards that water, so thirsty—
    he never intended to see.

    Athena, being Athena,
did not betray her wrath. Instead
    she asked him simply, "Who led you here?
What did he want from you? What
    could he have been thinking?"

He stood as straight as a column,
    and just as unable to speak—
as if he saw nothing at all.
    Then Coracle lost it. "What did you do,"
she cried, "O divinity, to my son?
    I thought we were friends. Human beings and gods can't be friends.
You stole his vision, or his reason. Dear son,
    my Tiresias, here's what I know has happened:
you saw the beautiful breasts,
    and the ribs and the hips of Athena
and now you will never know the sun again.
    Now I hate myself. I hate this terrible hill,
this Helicon. I thought I could be an exception,
    Athena's companion. What a price to pay
for a couple of hunting trips: my son's own eyes."

Then she took her son's hands, his beloved and motionless hands,
and made half-stifled, nearly melodic sounds,
    a kind of keening in the back of her throat.
She started to lead him downhill. But the goddess
    spoke to her: "Bring him back,"
she told her, "and try to get control of your words.
    For one thing, I haven't taken his sight away,
though people will think so,
    erring. If you want to know about blindness,
ask someone blind. Your son
    sees everything you see. But he can't pay attention,
because he's also seeing times to come.
    It's like having all
of everything, each pebble and sprig, each spray
    of rain or sun, press down on him at once.
He will know the past and the future.
    But he will need to be led from place to place.
That is his lot, and those are the laws
    of the universe, older
than I am, older than Zeus,
    and nothing can take them back.
You're still his mother. Have you heard
    of Autonoë? Do you know the name Autonoë?
Do you know how many burnt homages and prayers
    she has made, or how many she has yet to make?

No matter how many, she'll never get back her son,
    Actaeon, who ran after Artemis
until he saw her bathe,
    and that sight made him a hart for his dogs to devour.
He's a pile of bones in a box. Your son is your son,
    he's right here, and he's going to live a long life,
a life of rich work and a life of wise rewards,
    because you love him, and because I have loved you.
I will make him a prophet, a polyglot, a great explainer,
    admired by matchless tongues, in far-flung songs;
I will show him how to trace
    the singular path of every bird that flies,
how to tease out the omen in each one's call,
    each warble and wingbeat, each feather's barely
audible slice and trace of wind and sky.
    I will make sure he has followers in Boiotia,
an audience among the descendants of Cadmus,
    a role—not a tragic protagonist's role—in plays.
I will shape this cherry sapling as his perdurable staff,
    to help him keep track of his body
throughout his years as a master of sounds and words,
    and afterwards he will be the only spirit
who understands both the living and the dead,
    and they will keep honoring him under varying names.
In temples, in measures, he will be set apart."

Athena said so, and she never lies,
    although she may not reveal everything; she never lies,
Athena the daughter of Zeus. Here she comes now,
    as if I could see her, just as I did then.
Take up your stances. Sing her intricate odes.
    She knows how to make what she makes, and she will never lie.
O goddess, may you too find joy
    in everything you ride,
bringing your joy in turn to your faithful horses,
    when you go out with them and when you come home,
and if it pleases you,
    watch over the homes and the children here as well.

Acknowledgments

My thanks to the people who inspired this particular project, took care to encourage this project, worked on its behalf, or seemed to think it was a good idea, especially Mark Payne, Lauren Haldeman, Mark McGowan, Anne Savarese, Rosanna Warren and David Wilson-Okamura.

More thanks to allies and friends who saw drafts, read bits, gave advice, and bounced poems in progress off me, among them Cat Fitzpatrick, Carmen Giménez Smith, Rachel Gold, Illyana Rasputina, Catherine Rockwood, Jeff Shotts, Annie Staats, the Summers-Grey family, Rachel Trousdale, verity, and Monica Youn.

Thanks also to my colleagues at Harvard, especially to Nicholas Watson and Jorie Graham, and to the team at Blue Flower who have tried to keep me in the public eye. Additional thanks to the editors who have published and circulated these poems and parts of poems, sometimes in earlier versions.

And thanks, forever and for everything, to Jessica Bennett.

Epilogue to Callimachus

They will find pieces of me at Oxyrhynchus,
   some future Oxyrhynchus, on the Web.
      Whoever they are, they may wonder
whether my odd words and my awkwardness
   were unintended, or rather meant that way.
      They might go pretty far down the wrong track.
Unless I come back
   to tell them, they may never link us
      to all our pursuits. They won't be able to say—
at least, not with their usual confidence—
   what's a joke and what's a blunder,
      what's a stunt, and what's a flub.

Index of Greek First Lines

171

The Lockert Library of Poetry in Translation

† Out of print

The Man I Pretend to Be: "The Colloquies" and Selected Poems of Guido Gozzano, translated and edited by Michael Palma, with an introductory essay by Eugenio Montale

D'Après Tout: Poems by Jean Follain, translated by Heather McHugh†

Songs of Something Else: Selected Poems of Gunnar Ekelöf, translated by Leonard Nathan and James Larson

The Little Treasury of One Hundred People, One Poem Each, compiled by Fujiwara No Sadaie and translated by Tom Galt†

The Ellipse: Selected Poems of Leonardo Sinisgalli, translated by W. S. Di Piero†

The Difficult Days by Roberto Sosa, translated by Jim Lindsey

Hymns and Fragments by Friedrich Hölderin, translated and introduced by Richard Sieburth

The Silence Afterwards: Selected Poems of Rolf Jacobsen, translated and edited by Roger Greenwald†

Rilke: Between Roots, selected poems rendered from the German by Rika Lesser†

In the Storm of Roses: Selected Poems, by Ingeborg Bachmann, translated, edited, and introduced by Mark Anderson†

Birds and Other Relations: Selected Poetry of Dezső Tandori, translated by Bruce Berlind

Brocade River Poems: Selected Works of the Tang Dynasty Courtesan Xue Tao, translated and introduced by Jeanne Larsen

The True Subject: Selected Poems of Faiz Ahmed Faiz, translated by Naomi Lazard

My Name on the Wind: Selected Poems of Diego Valeri, translated by Michael Palma

Aeschylus: The Suppliants, translated by Peter Burian

C. P. Cavafy: Collected Poems, Revised Edition, translated and introduced by Edmund Keeley and Philip Sherrard, edited by George Savidis

Foamy Sky: The Major Poems of Miklós Radnóti, selected and translated by Zsuzsanna Ozsváth and Frederick Turner†

La Fontaine's Bawdy: Of Libertines, Louts, and Lechers, translated by Norman R. Shapiro†

A Child Is Not a Knife: Selected Poems of Göran Sonnevi, translated and edited by Rika Lesser

George Seferis: Collected Poems, Revised Edition [English only], translated, edited, and introduced by Edmund Keeley and Philip Sherrard

Selected Poems of Shmuel HaNagid, translated by Peter Cole

The Late Poems of Meng Chiao, translated by David Hinton

Leopardi: Selected Poems, translated by Eamon Grennan

Through Naked Branches: Selected Poems of Tarjei Vesaas, translated and edited by Roger Greenwald†

The Complete Odes and Satires of Horace, translated with introduction and notes by Sidney Alexander

Selected Poems of Solomon Ibn Gabirol, translated by Peter Cole

Puerilities: Erotic Epigrams of "The Greek Anthology," translated by Daryl Hine

Night Journey by María Negroni, translated by Anne Twitty

The Poetess Counts to 100 and Bows Out: Selected Poems by Ana Enriqueta Terán, translated by Marcel Smith

Nothing Is Lost: Selected Poems by Edvard Kocbek, translated by Michael Scammell and Veno Taufer, and introduced by Michael Scammell, with a foreword by Charles Simic

The Complete Elegies of Sextus Propertius, translated with introduction and notes by Vincent Katz

Knowing the East, by Paul Claudel, translated with an introduction by James Lawler

Enough to Say It's Far: Selected Poems of Pak Chaesam, translated by David R. McCann and Jiwon Shin

In Hora Mortis/Under the Iron of the Moon: Poems, by Thomas Bernhard, translated by James Reidel

The Greener Meadow: Selected Poems by Luciano Erba, translated by Peter Robinson

The Dream of the Poem: Hebrew Poetry from Muslim and Christian Spain, 950–1492, translated, edited, and introduced by Peter Cole

The Collected Lyric Poems of Luís de Camões, translated by Landeg White

C. P. Cavafy: Collected Poems, Bilingual Edition, translated by Edmund Keeley and Philip Sherrard, edited by George Savidis, with a new preface by Robert Pinsky

Poems Under Saturn: Poèmes saturniens, by Paul Verlaine, translated and with an introduction by Karl Kirchwey

Final Matters: Selected Poems, 2004–2010, by Szilárd Borbély, translated by Ottilie Mulzet

Selected Poems of Giovanni Pascoli, translated by Taije Silverman with Marina Della Putta Johnston

After Callimachus: Poems, translated by Stephanie Burt, with a foreword by Mark Payne